THE FUTURE
THE MOVIES

INTERVIEWS WITH MARTIN SCORSESE, STEVEN SPIELBERG, AND GEORGE LUCAS

THE FUTURE OF THE MOVIES

BY ROGER EBERT AND GENE SISKEL

Andrews and McMeel

A UNIVERSAL PRESS SYNDICATE COMPANY

KANSAS CITY

The Future of the Movies © 1991 by
Buena Vista Media, Inc.
Afterword © 1991 by Gene Siskel.
Introduction © 1991 by The Ebert Co.
For information write
Andrews and McMeel,
4900 Main Street,
Kansas City, Missouri 64112.

Library of Congress Cataloging-in-Publication Data

Ebert, Roger.
    The future of the movies / by Roger Ebert and
Gene Siskel.
        p.   cm.
    Interviews with Martin Scorsese, Steven
Spielberg, and George Lucas.
    ISBN 0-8362-6216-6 : $9.95
    1. Motion pictures—United States—Interviews.
2. Scorsese, Martin—Interviews. 3. Spielberg,
Steven, 1947- —Interviews. 4. Lucas, George—
Interviews. 5. Motion picture producers and
directors—United States—Interviews. I. Siskel,
Gene. II. Scorsese, Martin. III. Spielberg,
Steven, 1947- . IV. Lucas, George. V. Title.
PN1993.5.U6E24   1991
791.43'0233'0922—dc20   91-11450
                                            CIP

All royalties from this book will be donated
to The Film Foundation.

Attention: Schools and Businesses

Andrews and McMeel books are available at
quantity discounts with bulk purchase for edu-
cational, business, or sales promotional use.
For information, please write to:
Special Sales Department,
Andrews and McMeel, 4900 Main Street,
Kansas City, Missouri 64112.

CONTENTS

ACKNOWLEDGMENTS

Thanks are due to the "Siskel & Ebert" production team which produced the original "The Future of the Movies" TV special: Larry Dieckhaus, Jim Murphy, Andrea Gronvall, Sue Malone, and Carie Lovstad. And special thanks go to Stuart Cleland, for his expert transcription of the interviews. The project would have been impossible without the help of George Lucas, Martin Scorsese, Steven Spielberg, and their associates. And Donna Martin of Andrews and McMeel provided unfailing help and counsel.

INTRODUCTION
BY ROGER EBERT

Motion picture projectors are an ungainly invention, an arrange-
ment of gears and sprockets pulling a translucent film past a bright
light, while a shutter clicks furiously and a gizmo over to one side
turns squiggles into sound. The machines are typically housed in a
fireproof up under the rafters, reachable by a narrow stair and
inhabited by a projectionist who may be a movie lover but is just as
likely to be reading a paperback or looking at a baseball game on
his TV set. The film is delivered to him in heavy, battered cans
upon which someone has scrawled a few words of identification—
Indiana, reels 3–4—and usually he opens the cans in the right
order and feeds the film properly into his machines, but sometimes
he doesn't, and then the audience is treated to impromptu resur-
rections and premature proposals.

The audience. It sits in the dark, lined up facing the screen. The
light comes from behind their heads—from back there where dreams
come from. The movies are the most involving artistic medium ever
invented, the one that can temporarily preempt even our sense of
self, and give us the vicarious experience of being someone else,
somewhere else. Most of us have our first moviegoing experiences at
a young age, and our responses to the movies often echo that first
orientation. We sit passively in the dark and are told a story.

There have been many technological changes at the movies
since they were first invented. Griffith perfected the editing codes

and taught us how a closeup was related to the shots around it.
The movies began to talk. They began to be made in color. Their
screens grew wider, and sometimes the pictures could be in 3-D (or
what the ads claimed was 3-D). The things that could be done with
special effects grew more and more wondrous, until finally computers seemed able to fabricate almost any effect. The sound track
started to surround us. Movies came in 70 millimeter, and in the
vast Imax format.

And at the same time, of course, they were getting smaller, too.
Television shrunk them down to the size of a screen, and if they
were too wide it cheerfully chopped them from the left and right,
trimming them to fit. Movies on video were convenient, though,
and in recent years Americans have spent as much money to see
movies on various home screen formats as at the box office.

During all of this long process, however, the heart of the film
process remained unchanged: It depended on shining light
through a celluloid strip that was pulled along at a constant rate.
Movies were made up of still photographs, pulled past the light at
twenty-four frames a second. And no matter how much television
changed the rest of society, what went on inside a movie theater
was essentially unchanged.

Now it appears that video is poised to wage a final showdown
with its older and more aristocratic relative. High definition television will replace standard broadcast signals within a few years,
providing home pictures of much improved clarity and brilliance.
I saw high def demonstrated in December 1990 at the Hawaii Film
Festival, where technicians from Sony of Japan presented films shot
in the format. The picture was impressive. Ordinary TV has a sharp
falling-off at either end of the gray scale, but high def provided
darker darks and lighter whites and—most important—more subtle gray tones. The colors were truer, too, and bright reds and
oranges didn't bloom the way they do on conventional sets.

Not only was the quality of the picture better than anything I
had ever seen on TV, but the information in the signal was so much

richer that it could easily be projected across a room onto a really
large screen—one hundred or two hundred inches in diameter, say.
Front-projection TV already exists and is greatly improved in quality, but high def projection will be something else again, offering
consumers an approximation of a home movie screening room.
The boxy TV sets of the present may be replaced within a decade
by compact projectors hanging from the ceiling or hidden inside
a coffee table, projecting wall-sized images on big screens.

And yet . . . good as it is, does high def compare with the old
standard of light through celluloid? I don't think so. Film is still
the best medium for conveying moving visual information. Yet it
is so expensive and cumbersome, and video is so portable and so
responsive to uncertain lighting conditions! A 35-millimeter camera costs more than the average home, while portable video
cameras are consumer items. Traditional movies are expensive to
make, but the day is coming when features can be shot in high def
video by virtually anyone. How will this affect the future of the
movies?

This was a question that came up one night in September 1989
in Washington, D.C., where Gene Siskel and I had just attended an
anniversary celebration for the American Film Institute. Wandering
into our hotel bar later that evening, we found three of the honored
guests at the tribute sitting around a table together: George Lucas,
Martin Scorsese, and Steven Spielberg. They were having an
impromptu meeting to discuss The Film Foundation, an organi-
zation they founded to encourage the preservation of American
feature films—particularly those that are often neglected even in
the vaults of the major studios. As we talked, it was agreed that a
television special on "The Future of the Movies" might be a good
idea. We discussed several kinds of futures: The future of the art
form, the future of the technology, and preservation—the future
of old movies.

Three more formal conversations resulted. Siskel went out to
the back lot of the Universal Studios to talk with Spielberg at the

offices of his Amblin Entertainment. I visited George Lucas at Sky-walker Ranch, his sprawling complex in the Lucas Valley (no relation), north of San Francisco. And we both went to New York to talk to Martin Scorsese. The conversations resulted in a syndicated TV special in June of 1990, and now here are the edited transcripts of those conversations, showing three of the most influential directors of recent years taking a longer view about the medium they work in.

GENE SISKEL AND ROGER EBERT INTERVIEW MARTIN SCORSESE

ROGER EBERT: As somebody who likes to originate his own projects and who works more or less outside of ordinary conventions, is it going to be tougher for you in the nineties, even than in the seventies and the eighties?

MARTIN SCORSESE: I don't think so. I don't think so. I hope not as tough as it was in the beginning of the eighties. But it seems to me that the projects I have in mind are always only as good as the previous film. In other words, if your previous film has gotten some success, whether it's critical or hopefully financial, you pretty much might be able to get another "personal" movie made within the system. It was quite difficult for me in, say, '83, '84, '85, and '86. Those four years were very difficult.

EBERT: That was a period when a lot of American movies were very positive, you know.

SCORSESE: Yes.

EBERT: A lot of cheerleading, a lot of applause points, a lot of moments when the audience could share the triumphs of the heroes. And that is not really a strong point in your films.

SCORSESE: No. That's why I was amazed that I still keep getting to do some of them! And I always say that sometimes the best award you get is the fact that you get to make the picture at all. It's the nicest thing, you know.

EBERT: This is amazing for me to hear you say this, because you

1

were just voted by every single group that voted as the director
of the best film of the 1980s, *Raging Bull.*

SCORSESE: Yeah.

EBERT: Many people who voted on the films of the 1970s felt that
Taxi Driver was the best film of that decade. And yet you're
talking about how hard it is to get a new project going unless
your most recent film has been successful. But now you're not,
like, seventy-five years old! You're young—forty-eight. There's
nobody else in this country who has a better reputation, and yet
it's hard for you to get pictures made.

SCORSESE: The material is difficult. *The Last Temptation of Christ*
was difficult material. I mean, you have to give it that. It really is
a problem. We tried to do it once with Paramount and it was a
problem. It was a serious problem. The only way we could get it
made was, of course, to make it for $7 million in Morocco, inde-
pendent, and it was picked up by Universal. It seemed to get
enough good reviews. I was supposed to make *GoodFellas*—it
was originally called *Wiseguy*—first and then we finally got the
money to do *Last Temptation,* so we went ahead and did that.
But Warner Brothers was really very high on that book by Nick
Pileggi, *Wiseguy,* and they liked the script. And along with some
good critical reaction to *Last Temptation,* that gave us some—
not a lot, not a lot [laughs]—but some credence in Hollywood
to make *GoodFellas.* Because again it's a tough story. It's a tough
picture. It's a tough film. Even then, Bob De Niro came in on the
picture and that helped get the film financed.

GENE SISKEL: We can all understand why you would have pressure on
Last Temptation of Christ—moral-rights groups. What about
intellectual pressure from the people who give you the money
to make such films? What's the status of the executive suite that
you run into?

SCORSESE: So far it's been pretty good: At Universal it's been very
good for me, as well as at Warner Brothers, with this new film.
Fox really seems to want to make pictures with me, make my

kind of picture in that sense. Hopefully not ones that are going to cause as much of a stir as *Last Temptation* in that regard, because there's a lot of energy that goes into it and a lot that's wasted.

SISKEL: But what do they stop you from doing? What do they say? "No, do it this way"? I mean, we hear all the time that they want happy endings on pictures. You're not a happy ending kind of guy.

SCORSESE: No, no. It depends, again. It depends if you could have what I like to call a realistic ending on a picture. You know, a couple of name stars would help. A couple of big names in the picture would help.

SISKEL: That's your insurance policy?

SCORSESE: To a certain extent, yeah. And also people I like to work with, too. And a certain style of making the picture. I really think that when they finally see the near-to-finished product, that's when they usually are really won over. I hope that's the case.

EBERT: The financial journalists who write about the business seem to feel that in the nineties there are going to be fewer players. There've been all these conglomerations, takeovers, mergers, and so forth. There are fewer places in town to take a project. And also it seems to me that there's even more pressure to have a big star attached to a project.

SCORSESE: Yeah, I think so.

EBERT: You probably would find it very difficult to make a film now with no stars in it at all.

SCORSESE: It is. Yes, it is difficult.

EBERT: *Mean Streets* had no stars at the time it was made.

SCORSESE: *Mean Streets* didn't have any, it's true.

EBERT: So in the decade to come are you going to have to adjust to that reality or how are you going to react to it?

SCORSESE: Hopefully, the subject matter could handle the names. You see, that's the idea. If all the elements come together and it clicks, that would be wonderful.

EBERT: You mean in other words, if you have a good enough story, you could sell it on the story.

SCORSESE: Not necessarily a good enough story. If it's a certain kind of story that a star could fit in and doesn't overbalance the film in the wrong way, or it doesn't become a vehicle, in the wrong sense, a vehicle. That's the trick: to try get all the pieces together. In the case of *GoodFellas* we have Ray Liotta and Lorraine Bracco and Joe Pesci and Bob De Niro and Paul Sorvino. Bob's name gave us kind of a balance there with the studios. Also I think it's the first picture I've made with him since '81—nine years—so that it was kind of a reunion, and I think that helped give us the support we needed.

SISKEL: How does all the video money translate, in either giving you freedom or freeing up the medium of filmmaking?

SCORSESE: I always feel that it's pretty good. I still think, for example, that if you really want to make something badly enough and you can work it into a budget of $7 million or $8 million or $9 million, there's a good chance of getting it made. Maybe not by a major; independently, I'm talking about. And that's mainly because of the cable and the video rights.

EBERT: Are cable and video also turning into a star-dominated area, though?

SCORSESE: I don't know. I don't see it so much as star-dominated; rather, genre-dominated—you know, action pictures, comedies, romances, etc. There's so much out there. Pictures that come out like *My Left Foot* and other films that are really small-scale productions still seem to have an outlet in the theaters, which is really very helpful for the next decade.

SISKEL: In terms of genres and your future, what haven't you done that is on your checklist?

SCORSESE: Romance! [Laughter] Well, an unhappy romance, but it's a romance. Unrequited love.

SISKEL: There's unrequited love throughout all your pictures.

SCORSESE: Well, this will have costumes! This is 1870s. [More laughter]

SISKEL: Really?

SCORSESE: Yeah.

EBERT: Are you serious?

SCORSESE: Yeah. It's a nice project. I hope to do it in a couple of years; soon, I hope.

SISKEL: I've often thought that costume dramas are by far the toughest category to do successfully.

SCORSESE: I know, but the subject matter, especially this one, in terms of the passion that's held in restraint, creates so much tension in the story. And with the right cast and the right look to it, it might be very nice.

EBERT: What's the story? Where's it going to take place?

SCORSESE: It's New York, 1870s.

EBERT: Based on a book?

SCORSESE: A book, yeah. [Laughs] I'd rather not say. That's one thing. And I really hope one day, maybe in this decade, to have one of my pictures make a lot of money! That would be great.

SISKEL: That *would* be a different genre.

SCORSESE: That would be a different genre, especially if it makes a lot of money! They make some money, but these figures are amazing, aren't they? The picture comes out, and if it only makes $160 million they get upset! [Laughs]

EBERT: If you were looking at the way movies are going, though, in terms of the so-called home-run picture, the $200 million picture, the $300 million picture, do you think that's bad? Is that going to be bad in the next ten years, that so many studios seem to be swinging for the fences?

SCORSESE: I think it could be. It's difficult and that's why I think in a way I would need some names to help get certain kinds of stories I want made. Because the stories are no way, in the studios' eyes, going to aim for that level of $200 million receipts. Pictures like that are fascinating to me. It's the kind of picture I like to go into a theater and see on a wraparound screen, sit in the second row, and have incredible sound, and it makes $200 million! It's terrific.

EBERT: Do you think you can make a picture like that, congenitally?

SCORSESE: I don't know if I can.

EBERT: Do you have a popular imagination?

SCORSESE: You see, that's the thing. I like to watch them. I don't think I can do it. Especially all those special effects! [Laughs] I always have a dream: Imagine if you could really get a story that would fit that sort of thing. Both coexist, you know? That would be really nice. But I think you're right, that's the problem. I don't have the imagination. I am the audience. I'm the one who wants to be entertained. I'm the "them."

EBERT: You're constantly being thwarted by the black seed of an artist in your soul.

SCORSESE: Yeah, somebody there who's changing everything I do! [Laughs]

EBERT: The person inside there somewhere that refuses to compromise, just when you know you should.

SCORSESE: I know! It's like the end of *New York, New York.* After George Lucas saw the rough cut, I said, "What do you think?" He says, "Well, if they go away together at the end you can add $10 million more to your box office." And [my decision not to make the ending "happier"] wasn't anything noble, either. It just didn't seem right for the story! And he was right.

SISKEL: What is it that somebody like Spielberg has? He's the home-run hitter of all time, of your age group. What does he have that you don't have in that way?

SCORSESE: I really think he has his hand right on the pulse of not only what the public wants but their fantasies. What they need. And what they needed in the late seventies. Well, '75 was *Jaws,* but I'm talking about *E. T.* and *Close Encounters* in the late seventies and early eighties. That fantasy, the sense of wonder, and the sense of real theatrical magic. It's the kind of thing I'd want to see, the kind of thing I grew up watching. It's like Disney, really, who had that. It's just so fascinating. But he really knows what they need.

SISKEL: You have fantasy sequences though, or characters who have fantasies, all throughout your pictures. I'm thinking of you sitting in the back of the cab in *Taxi Driver* and you're looking up at a window. That's your kind of power fantasy.

SCORSESE: That's the fantasy though, that if you cross that line between reality and fantasy you're mad, you're insane. That's the whole point. In a way it's kind of nice to keep pushing that line.

SISKEL: But that's the kind of fantasy you're really interested in.

SCORSESE: Yes. That's what I mean. It's kind of enjoyable to explore that area, that gray area where you're really acting out the fantasy. The character in the back seat in *Taxi Driver* does not act out that fantasy.

EBERT: He wants the taxi driver to act it out for him.

SCORSESE: Yeah, yeah. And he does.

EBERT: "Let the meter run, let the meter run. I don't care what it costs. I want you to watch this." You know, when you talk about Spielberg giving the public what they need, your films seem to me to be giving the public what *you* need. In other words, your best films are certainly ones you needed to make.

SCORSESE: Yeah.

EBERT: And that used to be when we all started out, let's say in the late sixties and early seventies, the things that the best directors were trying to do: They were trying to express their own vision. And I find that rarer and rarer. Is it going to come back in the nineties? There's this character in *Flashback,* Dennis Hopper, who says, "Compared to the eighties the nineties are going to make the sixties look like the fifties."

SCORSESE: Right! [Laughs]

EBERT: I don't know if that's true or not. I noticed already there are movies that are attacking big business, which was sacrosanct in the eighties. And what else is happening?

SCORSESE: I think it will change. I really think so. Now that that ground has been broken by Steve Spielberg and George Lucas and everyone, I think you're going to have that genre: the big picture that you take the family to and you go and enjoy as much as possible. But I think things are already changing for the "smaller" films, you know. Things are really changing. There are some fascinating independent pictures being made. The big trick will be, how many personal pictures can you get made within this system in Hollywood?

SISKEL: Will you continue to make TV commercials? And why do you do it?

SCORSESE: I did two for Italy. You go there, you have some good food. That's the main thing. Buy some clothes and have some good food.

SISKEL: But the standard reading would be that you need it, and of course we feel bad that you have to need it.

SCORSESE: Oh, it's true, it's true. I've got to go there. It's northern Italy, of course, but what can you do?

SISKEL: No, I'm thinking about the Armani commercial.

SCORSESE: Oh, you mean the two Armani ones. That's all I did was the two Armani commercials. One was in black and white, sort of a little homage to Bertolucci's *Before the Revolution* and that period of beautiful black and white photography, the early six-ties Italian films—*I pugni in tasca* by [Italian director Marco] Bellocchio and all that. And did it with Nestor Almendros. And then the next one was in color. But the two that I made, they can't sell anything! They're just little mini-movies or something! [Laughs]

EBERT: Did you explain this to Armani before you signed the contract?

SCORSESE: Yes, I tried! It's all style. But he knows that; he says, "Well, they're good little films." So that was the idea. I thought they were good little films, and actually I learned a lot from the second one. Michael Ballhaus shot that one with me, and I shot material that for a forty-five-second spot lasted about a minute and ten seconds. I said, "It's impossible, I can't take any more out." Well, you know, it was shaved away, frame by frame. And the shots were still powerful. And I sort of applied a similar thing—some people will say not enough, I'm sure—to *GoodFellas,* in tightening and cutting. But *GoodFellas* is a longer film. It's about two hours and fifteen or twenty minutes.

EBERT: Your films are not derivative. You're more like the workman saying, "Maybe I can use this screwdriver."

SCORSESE: In weaker moments though, I say, "What the hell do I know? I'm just taking stuff that I've seen before!" But in other moments—you put it much better than I could! [Laughs]

SISKEL: I remember once at the University of Chicago—this was the early seventies—George Cukor was giving a lecture and somebody asked him, "You know, in *Dinner at Eight* you have somebody come down a staircase and you pan a certain way. Why did you do that?" And he said, "I don't remember." And then he asked him another thing, and he said, "You know, I can't really remember. It's a long time ago." And then he finally said, "Look, you know, you're asking me questions about why you see these common things in my pictures. What happens is on the set that day, probably I said, 'I don't know what to do. Maybe I'll do it the way I did it before.' "

SCORSESE: Yeah, yeah. That's interesting though, coming from those guys. Those were really directors.

EBERT: I want you to assume that you have precognition and I want you to tell me what happened to you in the 1990s. How was it for you, Marty—the decade? Looking back from 2001?

SCORSESE: If I survive.

EBERT: What were the high points and the low points?

SCORSESE: The high points? I was hoping that the high points would be that I would be able to try out different types of films. As I

said, in one case a love story in a costume situation or really to
be given the grace to be able to try different types of pictures. I
mean, my new film, *GoodFellas,* is not necessarily that. In fact,
that's like the end of the trilogy of *Mean Streets, Raging Bull,*
and *GoodFellas.* And that's really another whole movie in a way.
But starting out the decade with that is just the opposite. But
there are a couple of more stories that we'll have with those
people. So maybe that will come by the end of the decade. But
again, that's from a different point of view. But throughout I
would love to be able to try some different things, rather than
staying with exactly the same stories or same types of characters. Inevitably if I do try different stuff it's going to have a
similarity in terms of characters. They might be in different
places. They might be in different times and that sort of thing.
But I have a feeling that I'm always going to be attracted to
similar stories. It'll be interesting. I tried it with *Alice Doesn't
Live Here Anymore.* I tried it there. And to a certain extent, I
tried it with *Color of Money,* too, but again that has all the
accoutrements of one of my movies: pool halls, guys in shark-
skin suits, and that sort of stuff. I think the same characters
will come in. They'll seep through. But a different style, different way. And also to explore, again, hopefully, sharpening up
visual literacy: to be able to tell a story even better with a
camera.

SISKEL: Before we leave your future in the nineties, you once told
me about this concept of the master image, of the single shot
that represents a whole film. You want to come up with a master
image that would sum up you. If I started grabbing film out of
your vaults you'd say, "Leave me this frame, because this is what
I stand for."

SCORSESE: Well, that's a hard one. I know I should say something
witty, but I can't.

SISKEL: I don't want you to say something witty. Well, let's take
Raging Bull, because it was voted the best film of the eighties
and it's certainly one that you're pleased with.

SCORSESE: Well, I think the opening title shot. The shot that's used
over the titles has that quality for me. The sense of desolation,
the sense of loneliness and that sense of that ring being in a way
not different from the kitchen or the bedroom or the living
room or the street. It becomes a symbol for all of that, and that
was the idea of him in the ring. I'd just seen a lot of still photos
of fighters in the ring. That's how I came up with the idea. That
sense of loneliness and the sense of isolation. Fighting out your
life, struggling to survive. And struggling to be what you think
may be a good person or a good man, you know.

EBERT: My notion would be that in *Taxi Driver* the master image
would be De Niro walking alone down the street underneath
the X-rated movie theater.

SCORSESE: Yeah. Yeah. That's what the poster became.

EBERT: I know, and the cover of the album. Desolation and loneliness once again.

SCORSESE: Yeah. Yeah.

EBERT: Your two favorite adjectives. I can see the movie ads now:
"Desolate. Lonely."

SCORSESE: "Come and be entertained. Come and get totally de-
pressed!" No, don't believe that. It's not depressing. [Laughs]

SISKEL: Well, that brings up the obvious question, could you do a
conventionally happy film? A love story. You didn't in *New
York, New York*? You couldn't do it then. Could you do it in the
nineties? Do you even think about it as a challenge? "I'm going
to make a movie where they're happy and walk off together at
the end?"

SCORSESE: Well, see, my answer to that is, is it really happy if they
walk off together at the end? You know what I'm saying? Is it
really happy? In other words, there could be happiness in other
ways. That would be the trick. That would be the insight to
have.

EBERT: They're happy by all the pain they've saved each other by
not leaving together!

SCORSESE: [Laughs] Or learning about it. Learning about it and living with it and accepting it and moving on. And experiencing maybe a little less of that pain by doing so. Growing a little, maybe, if that's the phrase you want to use. I don't know. But I would love to do pictures that are really wide-across-the-board entertainment things. I can't quite believe in certain stories. I mean, as I said before, I like to be entertained by them, but to actually do it and tell the actor that's what's going to happen . . . I did one. *Alice Doesn't Live Here Anymore* has that, has a nice little ending at the end. Although it ends with her and the boy walking away.

SISKEL: Who do you think is the happiest character, the most content, self-satisfied character you've created in one of your films?

EBERT: The son in *Alice Doesn't Live Here Anymore*.

SCORSESE: The son! [Laughs] Let's see. What have we got? What have we got? Searching around real fast, and *Raging Bull* is no good, no. Maybe Rupert [Pupkin—the Robert De Niro character in *The King of Comedy*], no? What do you think?

SISKEL: I thought that he is doing what he wants to do.

SCORSESE: He does what he wants to do and he's wonderfully mediocre at it, too, and that's what's so frightening about it. He's midrange, and less offensive that way to many people. But that's what I think. He goes about it quite badly, he goes about it the wrong way. But he does reach some sort of satisfaction. Even Alice—Ellen Burstyn's character—reaches some of it. When they embrace and kiss in the diner with everybody applauding is one thing. But it ends with her walking off with the boy and with a slight insecurity added in there. But of course it is a traditionally happy ending. That's what it was. They told me at the time, "The head of the studio wants a happy ending." They said, "You've got to do that. They don't want any desolation at the end!" I said, "All right, you've got it."

EBERT: They don't get to Monterey, but they make it to the Monterey Motel.

SCORSESE: That was an accident!

EBERT: Oh, sure it was an accident!

SCORSESE: It really was! I'm not kidding! I looked through the lens and I said, "Oh, that's great! Let's leave it! Let's leave it!" We couldn't take it away. What could we do?

EBERT: I want to get you into technology a little bit. If you're talking about independent films in terms of an independent spirit—films that you want to make, stories that you generate—you're almost always talking about budget. Because, as you said, at a certain price any film can probably be made.

SCORSESE: Yeah, right.

EBERT: There are two things that are going to happen in the nineties that might make films cheaper and distribution cheaper, and I want to get your opinion on both of them. The first is the notion of shooting on high definition television or shooting in cheaper television-based ways instead of with the expensive 35-millimeter equipment that is usually used. Is there a future there? Will these be movies if they're shot on video? Do you like the way they look when they're shot on video? Would you like to work in video?

SCORSESE: It's like the archivists say: "We'll have to see." [Laughs] We'll have to see if this is good archival material.

EBERT: But you're going to have to make your decisions before . . .

SCORSESE: The problem is, of what I've already seen—there were several films already shot in video, I don't know if it was high definition—I wasn't too impressed.

EBERT: *Julia and Julia.* [A 1987 English-language film shot in Italy with high definition equipment and then transferred to film for theatrical release.]

SCORSESE: *Julia and Julia,* yeah.

EBERT: That was shot in high def.

SCORSESE: I wasn't too impressed. But there's more on the way, and it keeps becoming refined and of course I think the country has to move into actual home viewing for home televisions. High definition, one form or another. And I can see no other way around it: A lot of films will eventually be made directly with high definition equipment. There are some problems though. It's a very different way of shooting, from what I understand. I don't know that much about it, but what I understood back in 1984, I think it was, or 1985, in Milan I saw a test of this *Julia and Julia*. It looked pretty interesting to me, but there are other ways of shooting. In other words the cinematographer is mainly in a van. It's a very different way of going about things. There were some problems with panning, simple panning.

EBERT: Because there's a little bit of a strobe?

SCORSESE: There's a little bit of a strobe, yeah.

EBERT: When you look at a high def picture, what do you see when you see it on a movie screen and what do you see when you see it on a television screen, with the director's eye—the eye that has spent thousands and thousands of hours in editing rooms looking at film a frame at a time?

SCORSESE: I haven't had that much experience with the high definition situation. I've seen a few demonstrations, and I saw *Julia and Julia*. I saw the film. I've seen it on television also, and it looked pretty good to me. I wasn't completely convinced, but again I never rule out the possibility—in this decade, too—of maybe doing a picture like that on this situation using high definition video directly. It just seems to me that it's a whole new modus operandi: The cinematographer's mainly in the van. There's a great deal that goes on on the set that has to do with camaraderie between people and just feeding off each other and giving a glance to your cameraman when something beautiful is happening in a scene, or you give each other a look and you know you've got the take. It's that kind of thing that you need, that I enjoy. If you can't enjoy it with the people, that's a problem. I have a feeling some of the technology may be taking away some of that closeness. Again, I'm open to any of it because it's exciting to see. You're speaking to a number of people about this high definition. It's going to get better and it's going to look better and in some cases they're saying it's going to look better than VistaVision, which was of course the best wide-screen process.

EBERT: Of course, what the studios are saying is, in addition to the broadcast standard high def that will come and that everybody will have, they might come up with a better high def to shoot movies on.

SCORSESE: Absolutely. Yeah, exactly.

EBERT: And when they do that they want to deliver them to theaters by satellite.

SCORSESE: Yeah.

EBERT: Instead of having these big cans of film carried around everywhere.

SCORSESE: Yeah. That's right.

EBERT: Now, what will that do to a Martin Scorsese movie? Will that get into more theaters, less theaters? Will it help the business by allowing a wider variety of films, or will the same film be beamed to every theater in the country?

SCORSESE: I'm an optimist about that. I think that there's room then for more pictures. Especially beaming them in from satellite. There's much more experimenting. I mean, there are a number of independent films being made now that are quite extraordinary, and that we're seeing mainly on video, but that I haven't seen in the theater.

EBERT: I want to ask one more question in the area of high def. You have in your living room right now a projector that projects television on a screen on the wall.

SCORSESE: A Sony, yeah.

EBERT: And you can look at a picture in your living room that is 16-millimeter size.

SCORSESE: That's right.

EBERT: And this is expensive equipment.

SCORSESE: Yes.

EBERT: But eventually it's going to be cheap equipment, because once they get those mass produced it's going to be cheaper to make a projector than to put a television and a screen inside a piece of furniture.

SCORSESE: Oh yeah, yeah. I see what you're saying, yeah.

EBERT: So that the average American household ten years from now will be able to look at a television picture that will be of almost movie quality, on a screen that is limited only by the size of the room. The average American family—not the wealthy people— will be looking at a picture that's eight to ten feet wide, and it may come in through satellite: pay for view. How will this relate to the willingness of people to go out of their home, to go to a movie theater, to overcome urban agoraphobia—this fear of crowds or of mixing with strangers? How will it influence the entire moviegoing experience as we grew up with it?

SCORSESE: As we grew up with it, I think that's gone. That's certainly gone. The nostalgia that we had of seeing certain types of genre films: seeing *Shane,* let's say, for the first time on its second run in the Loew's theaters, and a co-feature with it. And sitting through the co-feature and then seeing the main feature, all that sort of thing. All the films that were made to be "B" films on the bottom half of a double bill were quite extraordinary, and that kind of thing is gone now. But I think because of the way we are—human beings—there still has to be and there still will be room for pictures that will be a communal experience. And maybe these will be the ones that make $300 million or some-thing, and it'd be more like Steve and George's films. I don't know. And yet I really think that's part of it. Why do people still go to plays? Why do they go see *Les Miserables?* or *Phantom of the Opera?*

SISKEL: They like to get out of the house, for one thing.

SCORSESE: Yeah. You must say that the plays *Phantom of the Opera* and *Les Miserables* are technically quite extraordinary. And that's the fun of watching them, that's the enjoyment of it, to see what happens.

EBERT: It's like going to the circus.

SCORSESE: Yeah. Exactly.

SISKEL: Is there a piece of equipment that you would say, "I wish I could have this invented for me, because this would change the way I make movies?"

SCORSESE: Yeah, just a camera that moves and glances the way I do: the way I move my head. But I think it would be nauseating for the audience, because I want to move as fast as possible sometimes. Or walking through the streets here in New York, and the clarity with which you just move and see another image where you direct your glance. With the two gears on the camera it's never quite accurate enough for me. That's one of the problems with the Steadicam image, although I love it and I've used it a number of times. But to use it all the time, the edges of the frame are always jiggling a little bit. It's kind of unsettling, it's insecure, it's uncertain.

EBERT: But your camera is almost always moving anyway. Even in shots where the camera seems to be nailed down, if you looked very carefully . . .

SCORSESE: There's always creeping or something.

EBERT: There's always some creeping going on, in practically every single shot in all of your movies. Which I think adds to the voyeuristic involvement of the audience, because a moving camera, it seems to me, is always more involving than a stationary camera.

SCORSESE: Yeah, I can never really get it as precise as the way I want it, the way I see certain things occur.

SISKEL: As directors grow older, traditionally their shooting style gets more and more simple. More static shots. Where on the curve from a frenzied camera to, let's say, Jean Renoir, do you see yourself?

SCORSESE: I tried that! I tried that in *King of Comedy.* Everybody got mad. Nobody liked it! [Laughs] Well, that showed up on a number of lists too, though, as best of the decade, *The King of*

Comedy. The style: 1903, Edwin S. Porter. If you look at *King of Comedy* I think a lot of it works because it's like each frame is hermetically sealed. And these people are sealed inside this world of celebrity, and trying to get in there. And nobody can get in, you know. Rupert can't get in and it's tight. The more the frames are rigid, the more tension. The story just lent itself to that style. I tried that, but then I found that *when* to stop moving the camera is more important. If I think the way you're suggesting, if I say, "Well, if you look at the last films of Dreyer, if you look at the last films of Renoir, or even most of Renoir's stuff, or John Huston's *Wise Blood* and pictures like that," I think that I might give into something. In other words, it might become laziness on my part, and I have to really go through the process the way I normally go through it.

SISKEL: The worst kind of censorship is usually, for an artist, self-censorship—you don't push yourself. Although *you* push as hard as almost anybody in the movies today. Could you talk about a scene in your work that you now, in the future, would have done differently?

SCORSESE: No. Because the decision was made. Within the circumstances, that decision is the right decision. That's it. For that period of time and for that story and for that actor and for that cameraman, that's it.

SISKEL: You don't look back? When you saw *Taxi Driver* again?

SCORSESE: Only a couple of things in *Taxi Driver;* a couple of things I didn't get fast enough or I didn't move clearly enough. The business I was talking about before, about being rigid and being able to move the frame a certain way and picking up a piece of action. I just didn't stage it properly. That's a technical mistake. But the shot was right for that period of time. You can't go back and recut all your pictures and reshoot all your films. It's insane. The only thing you can do is say, "Look, that's the decision that was made at that time." If things don't come up exactly to what you had wanted it's usually a technical problem—a problem with using the wrong piece of equipment. Or we have no time; we've got to get out of there and we can't come back. Actor isn't feeling too well, etc. Not enough money, you know.

SISKEL: I asked you about a technological change that you'd like to see in the business. You talked about a camera, in theory. What about in the companies that make movies. If you were king for maybe a year, let's say, in Hollywood, what would you do? Would you start a writers' school? Would you go back to the old studio system? What would you want to change about the people and the system that you have to work in?

SCORSESE: It's difficult to say, because, again, I only make a certain kind of film. You're talking about if I was a different person completely.

SISKEL: No, you've been saying throughout that you'd like to see more independent kinds of pictures.

SCORSESE: What I would like to see is not necessarily more "personal" films, but an idea of a person who is visually literate, who knows how to tell a story with a camera, whether it's a television camera or it's a motion picture camera. And that doesn't mean that words go out the window, either. It doesn't mean no story, because you have to have a story. But I find that visual literacy is really lacking, and that's the thing that I think needs to be developed. You don't necessarily achieve that by trying to make certain films that make a certain kind of money. "Let's make a sequel to this." And this maybe is the fault of the film schools or maybe it's the fault of the film students, I don't know. I think the system is not allowing filmmakers to come through—male or female, whatever—that really know how to tell a story with a lens. And I think that has to do with the tyranny of a visually illiterate society. You know what I'm saying? Friends of mine always say that very often we see some really wonderful films, which on the level of their visual literacy are illiterate. [Laughs] If they were written we'd say they were terrible!

SISKEL: It wouldn't be grammatical.

SCORSESE: It wouldn't be grammatical; they wouldn't be able to express themselves. They wouldn't be able to express their emotions through the words if they were writers, the way they're shooting some of this stuff.

EBERT: The movies are shot on a visual style that would be the equivalent in words of "See Dick and Jane run," so to speak.

SCORSESE: That's right.

SISKEL: No! "See run Dick and Jane!"

SCORSESE: Even worse! [Laughs]

EBERT: Gene and I were looking at a movie earlier this week, directed by a man who is a studio chief and who has announced his retirement from directing in order to be a studio chief.

SISKEL: This is Joe Roth of 20th Century-Fox.

SCORSESE: Oh, yeah, Joe Roth.

EBERT: To mention a name. We observed to each other after the film was over that it did not contain a single interesting shot. Every single shot was simply the obvious setup to photograph that part of the screenplay.

SISKEL: The sort of pictures that we'd probably come up with if we were directing. Just put it in the center; it's like "Mom and Pop on vacation."

SCORSESE: But it's ironic. I haven't seen Roth's *Coupe de Ville* but it's ironic, because in a way at the same time that we're discussing this in terms of the system, people buy video cameras and they're all learning how to tell stories visually at home or make a point. Not even tell the story. "Tell the story" is the wrong phrase. But just to get across how to express yourself through an image, through a picture, like paintings. I think that that's the main thing. How do you teach that? I don't know how you teach that. I think what you have to do in this country is get more respect for it. It's the reason Hitchcock, let's say, never got an Academy Award. It's the same reason, because you couldn't take it seriously. "You couldn't take that seriously. Those are thrillers!" And, "Oh, he does fancy camera tricks." Fancy camera tricks!

Now look at that stuff! He knew how to tell a story—or make a point, I should say—with that lens and with the movement of the lens and where the actor comes into frame and is the actor in shadow or are the eyes lit? It's fascinating, and I think that to this day there's still not enough respect for it.

SISKEL: I agree with you that there's not enough respect. And I want to ask you, as you say it that way and with the teaching in schools, how would people learn how to shoot films if they don't study writing with the camera?

SCORSESE: That's the idea.

EBERT: Why don't people know how to see films? The audiences of the thirties and forties loved films that were very high in style.

SCORSESE: Yeah, yeah.

EBERT: Lots of tilt shots, shadows, strange camera movements. Today's films are often shot like television, and audiences don't seem to be bored by that.

SCORSESE: Mainly because I think a lot of the stories are pretty strong and some of the actors are just extraordinary, and that's it. They think that's enough.

EBERT: I want to ask you about one shot in one of your films that is apparently an extremely simple shot. Robert De Niro is being interviewed for a job as a taxi driver right at the beginning of *Taxi Driver.* There's a shot of him apparently from the point of view of the man who is the dispatcher. Then the camera moves closer to him.

SCORSESE: Yeah. It comes up.

EBERT: But what does it do? It's not a zoom. It comes up obliquely.

SCORSESE: No, it was a boom, a little boom. On the end a Mitchell dolly has a little bit of an arm that comes up, that the camera's on, and as we came up we moved in. It's a mini "crane in."

EBERT: It's almost vertiginous for the audience.

SCORSESE: Yeah, yeah.

EBERT: You came up and in, in a way that the camera was going in a different direction than simply closer to De Niro.

SCORSESE: Exactly.

EBERT: Now where did that come from? You're sitting there that day . . .

SCORSESE: No, no, it's not that day! I do those shots way in advance.

EBERT: You storyboarded the whole film.

SCORSESE: Yeah, I still do that.

EBERT: So you knew that you wanted to get closer.

SCORSESE: On those lines, on those lines exactly.

EBERT: On those very lines?

SCORSESE: Yeah. Only on those lines.

EBERT: Now, where did that come from?

SCORSESE: Somewhere, I don't know. I was working out the shots.

EBERT: There's another shot in Palantine's office where the camera's on tracks and it moves very quickly from the area of Albert Brooks's desk over to Cybill Shepherd's desk, but the camera is at an angle to the direction of the tracks. Do you remember that shot?

SCORSESE: I don't recall that. But I remember a lot of quick moves that I saw since I saw the film. As I said, I only saw the film when I was doing the commentary for the laser disc three weeks ago. I hadn't seen it since I made it. So I remember seeing two quick shots moving in toward her desk and I remember the speed of it that I wanted. I don't think we ever got those technically quite right, because it was a little bumpy, that shot. I remember Mike Chapman and I were a little concerned about it. I wanted to move almost like zooming in with your eyes on a person. But not with a zoom, because a zoom is different, as we know. We wanted the actual physical movement of a machine coming toward her.

EBERT: But it sidles past.

SCORSESE: It goes past, yes.

EBERT: In other words the camera doesn't move in the same direction that the tracks are moving.

SCORSESE: Right. Yeah, that's right.

EBERT: It's at an angle to the tracks.

SCORSESE: Yeah, I know that. As I said, all those shots were story-boarded. And then very often what happens is that when you get there, we might have had to add that move on because of certain limitations of the location, etc. And sometimes we came up with some interesting things that way. I think that that's the case with that shot. But the first one that you talked about was planned way in advance.

EBERT: Now how can that be taught?

SCORSESE: I don't think you can teach that. I think you have to be able to visualize in your head, and I think you have to be able to draw little pictures even if with stick figures to learn this, or to learn to express these feelings with pictures.

EBERT: In your book you show all the stick figures of one of the sequences in *Taxi Driver.*

SCORSESE: Yeah.

EBERT: But the thing is, you say, because you obviously believe it, that it's too bad that directors aren't being taught to think visually and that people aren't being taught to see visually. A professor in college in a short-story course that I took, once told me, "I don't know why I teach this course. Some of the students who come in here can already write short stories and always could, and the others will never be able to." And I think it's the same with directors, in a way.

SCORSESE: Exactly. I think so, too. And I don't know if they can be taught, but you can at least be encouraged in this society to express yourself visually. I think what's being encouraged is the opposite. It's too bad, because I don't think everybody's comfortable with it yet, even after the past fifty, sixty years. They're not comfortable with it yet. It's very difficult. I think it's harder to tell. Again, Hitchcock is a perfect example of that: not really being appreciated by Americans, in the mid-sixties, late sixties and through the seventies, until today. We just showed *The Birds* on the weekend to my friend's son, who's nine years old.

And it's so wonderful to be able to show that film or films like that; we showed *Wagonmaster* also—Ford. But to see a kid, to watch someone experiencing that for the first time! And especially the fact that it has no answers! [Laughs]

SISKEL: Can I go back to the idea of the enemies of visual literacy? The one that we haven't talked about is television.

SCORSESE: That's the funniest thing because now, MTV and all these images that come flying across are hopefully inadvertently teaching younger people to be able to understand images— emotionally, intellectually understand images, but again that's something you can't teach. You can't teach it. Either you have it or you don't have it: to be able to use images in that way. But it seems to me that television should be making it easier for visual literacy, and it doesn't seem to be. It doesn't seem to be, but it should be.

SISKEL: There's nothing literate about prime-time.

SCORSESE: I don't watch it. I really don't watch that. I usually watch films and music.

SISKEL: We don't watch it, and we're the "movie people," or "movie lovers." We don't watch it.

SCORSESE: Yet the "Miami Vice" style, the look of that film.

EBERT: Yeah, and "Moonlighting."

SCORSESE: "Moonlighting," the look was quite good.

EBERT: But those series were very, very expensive to shoot and took a long time.

SCORSESE: Really?

EBERT: When they're grinding out half an hour every week, on the same set, there's very little you can do visually.

SCORSESE: I know, I know.

EBERT: And so people get accustomed, I think, to "insult" comedy with a laugh after every line.

SCORSESE: Right.

EBERT: And the camera just stays there and looks at them.

SCORSESE: Right. In a funny way television itself is a different thing.

I have it on all the time and every now and then I look at an image. If I'm really going to look at a film on television, I'm going to sit down, turn the lights out and look at a picture. Look at a film, a motion picture. Maybe the images have become like junk images, in a way, like junk mail. And that's unfortunate.

SISKEL: And the attention span.

SCORSESE: Oh, attention. That's the hardest thing. That's the hardest thing. I think audiences today have to have a picture that moves so fast and they have to have, not necessarily the story moving fast, but a lot of cuts. A lot of cutting, you know.

SISKEL: Their eye isn't trained as yours was in school to look around the frame of the picture.

EBERT: Well, there aren't any repertory houses for people to go to either, in order to look at old movies.

SCORSESE: No, there's one in New York now, the Biograph. I think.

EBERT: One. There used to be six.

SCORSESE: There used to be six. I know. Yeah.

EBERT: Are you trying to tell us something?

SCORSESE: The Biograph. But it's lost, because there are no repertory houses, nothing. So it's gone.

SISKEL: What could people do at home to see movies better?

SCORSESE: To see better in terms of viewing the film?

SISKEL: To see films better. You've a chance to say, "Here's how I look at pictures."

SCORSESE: Oh, you mean the actual viewing experience of a picture, especially at home.

SISKEL: I mean it both ways. I mean seeing it at home and then I mean seeing what you have created.

SCORSESE: I don't know. I don't know if any audience member is really going to be able to tell, "This is making me feel a certain way because of the move to the left, and you didn't expect to see that other figure come in from the right, and then the camera zooms there—it's not a track, it's a zoom." I don't think an audience is ever going to know that. The only hope you can

have for that would be that they feel the effect of it, and say,
"Boy, I liked that part where that happened." And if they're
interested enough they can go back and study it. That's one
of the wonderful things about laser now, laser disc and video.
They can go back and study how that happened and what
made you react that way. For example the opening sequence of
David Lean's *Great Expectations*. At New York University they
used as an example *Odd Man Out* and *Great Expectations*.
And they showed you the opening sequence of *Great Expectations* when Pip comes from the grave and moves this way
and suddenly Finlay Currie comes in—Magwitch, I guess.
They played that back a number of times, reprinted in slow
motion to show the effect and how the editor worked and how
the camera was placed in such a position to create that effect.
And that's for people who are really interested to learn that
sort of stuff and understand why they felt that way. It was one
of the better examples that we had at the time. The only thing
I think you can hope for is to really have an audience watch
your movie—if they're going to watch it at home—usually in
a darkened room and without too many interruptions, and
have them open to it so they can experience these emotional
effects. That's the idea.

EBERT: You wrote an article for *Video Review* in which you said that
as long as the movie that you have made is available in some
video format in the width that you made it you now feel free to
go back to working with a real wide screen.

SCORSESE: Well, I never use wide screen. I love wide screen, because
I was twelve years old when I saw *The Robe* in wide screen and
stereophonic sound at the Roxy in New York. When that curtain
opened and that screen was big, that was great. We had seen
panoramic screen a few years earlier; *Shane* in a panoramic
screen was quite good. But that sense of wonder, I think, was
part of the reason I always wanted to make movies, that sense of
magic when the curtains open and that screen is so enormous.

However, of course, the kind of pictures I make don't necessarily lend themselves to stereophonic sound. But I fell in love
from 1953 to 1960 with the compositions of the wide screen,
the anamorphic screen. I really did, and I would always love to
have done that but I never shot a film wide screen because of
what it did on TV.

EBERT: They chop it back.

SCORSESE: Yeah, they chop the sides.

EBERT: Now let me ask you about this in terms of the decade ahead,
the nineties. Wide screen on a regular television screen has to
be compromised somehow.

SCORSESE: Letterboxed, yeah.

EBERT: You either have to letterbox it or you have to lose part of it.
Now we're going into a period where over the next ten years
people will find in their homes a wide screen television set.

SCORSESE: Now the problem will be the opposite.

EBERT: They'll take the top and bottom off.

SCORSESE: Top and bottom off *Monsieur Hulot's Holiday,* so you'll
lose all the jokes—you'll lose all the sight gags. Or Chaplin—
you'll lose his feet. You'll lose the sight gags! [Laughs]

EBERT: Assuming they don't do that but they letterbox it this way
[Roger indicates the sides of the wide screen television would be
masked].

SCORSESE: Letterbox the sides. That's easier to take, I think, for most
people, letterboxing on the sides. I love the letterboxing that's
being done. Especially on the laser discs, I think it's quite
beautiful.

EBERT: But let me ask you this: When television and video came in
as a very important financial aspect of movies, directors were
told to stop using the real wide screen. The old CinemaScope.

SCORSESE: Right.

EBERT: And let's get narrower. Now with the TV screen like this, if
you letterbox a little bit you're back to CinemaScope again.

SCORSESE: That's right.

EBERT: Are you going to find pressure on you now to shoot in wide screen whether you want to or not?

SCORSESE: Well, you see I'd like to. I would love to shoot everything in wide screen.

EBERT: You'd like that pressure.

SCORSESE: I would like to shoot everything in wide screen at this point. The thing about it is that I think certain stories are meant for it, others are not. But I think with that coming in—that which you just described—you'll also be able to use the wide screen in more obvious compositions. What I mean by obvious is actually utilizing the wide screen, whereas now many films are made in Panavision, where the action is still kind of in the center so that when it gets to TV sometimes you can't even tell it was wide screen. But I would really like to use it so that you make use of the wide screen the way that they did in the fifties and early sixties. And I have a feeling that you can make any story really for the wide screen. Remember all the French new wave films that were wide screen? Intimate pictures were still intimate. *Jules and Jim,* you know.

SISKEL: We're all talking about movie images that have lasted, the ones that you have made. Now we want to talk about how to keep those images alive. What is the status of film deterioration right now?

EBERT: I want to just give you a prop. This is a can from the Columbia vault that they found when they went looking for *Lawrence of Arabia.* This is the condition that the film can was in. [Hands him battered film can.]

SCORSESE: God.

EBERT: One of the cans in the vault.

SCORSESE: Well, yeah, this is it.

EBERT: They were all in equally bad shape.

SCORSESE: Well, this of course is an extreme. This is an extreme situation of 65-millimeter film and this is what happens. You have to understand: There was a period in the late sixties and early seventies in Hollywood where it was before video, with lots of changes in studio heads and that sort of thing—administrations—and the last thing in the world they could think of what was in the vault. What was in the vault should be okay. They're finding out now and they are becoming more aware of it because, with video and laser disc and satellite soon, and all of that, the vault is really corporate assets. It's their corporate assets. If not *the* most important thing, it's the second most important thing. The first thing is of course the productions that they make each year. But the idea would be, what about all the old stuff. Because that's where all the money really is going to come from. Steve Spielberg, George Lucas and myself, Woody Allen, Robert Redford, and Sydney Pollack and Francis Coppola—we have a group that we've tried to form now, a foundation which will try to be sort of a bridge between archives and the studios. So far in our discussions with studios, especially Warner's and Columbia and Universal, they have become more aware of this problem. And I think their commitment is going to be quite interesting, in the next few years. A continuing commitment to cleaning up everything in the vaults. CRI's [Color reversal intermediates] aren't very good; maybe make new internegatives on certain titles. In the case of 65-millimeter films, one of the reasons I think *Lawrence* is this way is that there were so many cuts on the film. There were so many strange things that happened after the film opened. And 65-millimeter, well, how many prints are you going to strike from the 65-millimeter? On re-releases they probably only struck them from a 35-millimeter CRI. So naturally, and again with all the changes in studio administration, it's difficult. But Columbia only has two more films, I think, that were made in 65-millimeter: *Lord Jim* and *McKenna's Gold*. And they now are looking at that and making sure that the negative is somewhat restored. But they have become more aware—and I think with our help—of how much these things mean to us because it is the

end of the century now. It's the last decade. This is the art form
of the century. It's American. And this whole hundred years is
like a Golden Age. Forget the thirties and the forties and the
fifties. People in 2050 are going to look back at this century
as the Golden Age of Cinema, not only in America but everywhere else: certain kinds of films being made. And we're the
ones right now, in Hollywood, filmmakers and the studios and
the archives—who are going to get caught with the rap if we
don't take care of them! They're going to say, "Why didn't they
do anything about it?" We're "they" in that way.

EBERT: The films that are being made now are going to be preserved.

SCORSESE: Yes.

EBERT: In other words, preservation of current films is now taken
care of because of the value of the films on video.

SCORSESE: Yes. Yes. Absolutely.

EBERT: So then we have the restoration of films that may be in
various states of decay to still worry about.

SCORSESE: That's right, even films up to the early eighties. I mean
Steve Spielberg is rejuvenating *Jaws* right now. As I said, Universal is very strong on this right now. The only reason I haven't
mentioned the other studios is I haven't discussed it with them
yet, personally. But in the next few weeks I hope to do that.

EBERT: You're especially interested in the preservation of color.

SCORSESE: Yeah.

EBERT: In the sense that the film can still be there and the color is
faded out of it.

SCORSESE: Right.

EBERT: You've talked about it a lot.

SCORSESE: Well, that was a specific problem only from 1953 to 1980.
Only thirty years! [Laughs] That's only thirty years, everybody!
Everything made from 1953 to 1983 or 1984 and printed on a
certain kind of stock at that time, after six or seven years or
maybe twelve years in certain cases would fade to a pink or red.

And I always felt that it was really bad because it affected the actual storytelling. It affected the emotion that you were supposed to feel or the intellectual idea that you were supposed to have when you saw certain images, because the image was hardly there. It affected the actors; the actors' faces would fade away into the sky and you couldn't see their eyes. It's one of the reasons I did *Raging Bull* in black and white; that's one of the reasons. Since I talked about that around the world, I used the trip opening of *Raging Bull* in different countries around the world to bring this to the attention of the filmmakers and the archives. The archives knew about it; the studios and the filmmakers didn't quite understand it. And Eastman Kodak has since then made available at no extra cost a low-fade stock which lasts, they feel, anywhere from eighty to one hundred years. So it's pretty good. Granted, you may get an old print of a film that was made in 1985 or 1986, and it will be splicey and scratched because it's been projected too many times, but the color will always be there. Not as vibrant as the old three-strip Technicolor IB, but again that's a nostalgia thing as a child growing up and seeing those Technicolor films. It's a certain style of filmmaking, a certain style of using color that came around 1936. Natalie Kalmus-style. [Natalie Kalmus, former wife of the president of Technicolor, served as a consultant on Technicolor films.]

EBERT: The colors were brighter then, right? There's this restoration that was done, for example, on *She Wore a Yellow Ribbon*.

SCORSESE: Oh, it's supposed to be great. I haven't seen it yet.

EBERT: Where they saturated the color again. But didn't you complain, though, about Ted Turner's version of *Gone with the Wind?* That he didn't bring it back to Technicolor, he toned it down for modern tastes.

SCORSESE: Yeah, that bothered me only because, I mean, the color is still quite extraordinary, but I felt why is a modern taste bluer or cooler? Why can't it be warmer? Maybe they think today that the use of color three-strip at that time was more candy-colored, more for musicals. And that's what color was used for at that time. Although one of the great film noirs that was made in color: *Leave Her to Heaven* was made in three-strip Technicolor. It was quite extraordinary. But at that time I think they were warmer and prettier because of the subject matter of the films. And maybe they feel now with *Gone with the Wind* that they had to lighten it up a little bit or cool it out a little bit. I prefer the original intention of the cinematographer and the director, and in that case really Selznick, the producer of the picture, who made it.

SISKEL: The problem would appear that, as we talk now, films that you would like to save are dying.

SCORSESE: Yes. Part of the problem will be—even now that the studios are beginning to realize this and they're beginning to really do some serious preservation work with the archives and restoration work—there's so much in the vaults and where do you go first? I was hoping with the archives to come up with some sort of direction as to which titles to deal with first on a yearly basis, going back to the silent films for each studio. That's the next step that we're trying.

SISKEL: Are you going to try literally to work from the oldest to the newest?

SCORSESE: Not necessarily. This all has to be worked out with the archives, and the archives have to tell us which seem to be in danger, or what about nitrate? What about all the stuff that's in nitrate? I know archival work at UCLA right now: Eighteen million feet of nitrate newsreels. Now, it's a dollar a foot to transfer it to acetate film, so that's $18 million, and they don't have it. Where can you get it? Especially for newsreel. And of course, I often think that newsreel is as important obviously as regular features. So what Bob Rosen of UCLA told me is that they're attempting to transfer a lot of the nitrate onto digital video. So that at least there'll be a record of it. And maybe, maybe, maybe in the next decade some more money will come through to transfer this historical footage, which is really the most important thing.

SISKEL: What about a preservation tax? A dime a ticket?

SCORSESE: Oh, yeah. Well, that's one thing. But I think what's interesting about the studios now—and they're beginning to realize this—is it's really their films, the films that they own. They have to start making sure that their product is still there, that they have something to sell! If it just decomposes, they're in a lot of trouble. So a lot of money from the studios, I hope, will start going into their own vaults, their own corporate assets. The other problem is: A lot of libraries are sold, and you find that films that were once made at Universal or at Paramount, let's say, have been sold to a smaller company somewhere, and that guy's now out of business. And he sold it to someone else, and it literally gets lost. That's one of the things this foundation is going to do: We're going to try to find titles. It usually comes down to calling up and finding a person and begging them to go into the vault. And they say, "I can't. I have a lunch at two o'clock, and I have to leave." It really comes down to dealing with the bureaucracy of the situation. Some of the people you find, by the way, who are working in administration in these smaller companies really are dedicated to it and they really love the idea and they'll do it for you. But other people, what do they care? They don't care.

SISKEL: You met with the head of Sony in America recently on preservation.

SCORSESE: Yeah.

SISKEL: Were you pitching him for money for your group?

SCORSESE: No. The idea is that the studios should give the money to themselves. [Laughs] That's the idea. It's their money. It's their corporate assets. What do I want out of it? I want to see the movies. That's all. I want to see them. I want to see them ten years down the line, when everybody's still alive. We look at them, and suddenly they look like brand-new copies and it's gorgeous. That's what I want to see. That's for me. But I also want other generations to see them. That's the idea.

EBERT: Now, you're against colorization.

SCORSESE: Well, yes.

EBERT: Of course. But, what about using colorization technology to restore color and to conceal scratches and splices?

SCORSESE: That's possible I think.

EBERT: For example, if two frames are missing, that technology could put those two frames back in on video.

SCORSESE: If two frames are missing in the negative, yeah. Absolutely. There's so much George Lucas can tell you all about that. He's got that somehow worked out. [Laughs] The computer gets me nervous. I have no idea how to touch it or what to do with it but I think it can be helpful. There's some cases that certain negatives are completely faded, completely gone. Well, some computer enhancement would help them, because it was a color film originally. I think it can be used for certain things like that. But again, in many of the cases you'll find that a lot of the films that are faded are minor films, "B" films. Nothing's minor to me. I still want them fixed. But in a case like some fifties Allan Dwan pictures, let's say, because some of them were made in a kind of a cheap color process like TruColor the negative is in bad shape. It's a very hard sell to tell somebody to redo a "B" Western and to spend, what?—$50,000 to $60,000 or $100,000 just to put the color back in. It's a hard sell! That's if everything else has been saved and taken care of, then you can get to that, I think. I would love it. I love the Allan Dwan stuff of the fifties. I adore it. And a lot of those prints are still around, by the way, some of the ones he made: *Slightly Scarlet* and *Cattle Queen of Montana,* I think was it, and a few others. *Tennessee's Partner* was a wonderful film and a lot of prints are around, and you can get the original color. I like them. John Alton photographed them. Alton was that great cinematographer of *T-Men,* and won

the Academy Award for the ballet in *American in Paris.* Our
thing is with this foundation. You've got to ask George and
Steven about it also.

SISKEL: We will.

SCORSESE: Because they're part of it. We're trying to be like a bridge
between these two groups. However, first things first. Start
restoring, start preserving the negatives. That's the main thing.
And then, of course, start working in conjunction with the
archives. Have double elements, so that you have different printing elements, not just in one place, because fires destroyed
Citizen Kane, the original negative of that. It's a lifetime work.
As we get along it's going to be making sure film students can
see pictures in 16-millimeter in the university. The older films
especially. Maybe some of the new stuff like *Lethal Weapon* they
could see on video. That's okay, because it was made with a
different thing in mind, different outlets. But they have to see
The Big Heat. They should see it on a screen. Fritz Lang. Even
though it's plain black and white, you know. You get a sense of
that frame and long takes.

March 15, 1990

GENE SISKEL INTERVIEWS STEVEN SPIELBERG

GENE SISKEL: What do you have planned for yourself in the near future?

STEVEN SPIELBERG: Nothing. [Laughs]

SISKEL: That's not true.

SPIELBERG: Not much.

SISKEL: If you stopped right now, wouldn't you have three or four years of projects to take up your time?

SPIELBERG: Not really. No. I pretty much cleaned out my drawers during the decade of the eighties. And everything that I had stored away in the seventies that I hadn't made yet—*E.T.*, which was a stored away bottom-drawer project from the seventies—I made in the eighties. I pretty much cleaned out the locker. I've got some old smelly tennis shoes in there somewhere but there's not a plethora of old adolescent ideas just waiting and urging me to fulfill the commitment.

SISKEL: And those were adolescent ideas that you've made and realized. Where are you going to get the stuff to fill up a new drawer? Where is it going to come from in life? You live in a very sheltered community in Los Angeles. At least we from the Midwest and East think so.

SPIELBERG: Well, I think the general perception is that everybody who lives in Los Angeles and makes movies exists in a partial vacuum. And you know, the fact is, it's not true at all. Life is life no matter where you live. And I travel and I enjoy myself, and that's where all movie ideas come from, just day-to-day living.

SISKEL: What have you seen that you've said, "This could be . . ."? Let's just be speculative.

SPIELBERG: This could be a . . . ?

SISKEL: "This could be a feature film." Or, "There's something that I've been noodling around. This is possible."

SPIELBERG: Well, it's no secret that I am interested in a biography of Howard Hughes. I've been working with Warren Beatty and Bill Goldman on a possible Howard Hughes biography.

SISKEL: What attracts you, other than he's a weird guy?

SPIELBERG: Oh, he's beyond being weird! I mean, he was really just a complete contradiction. Here was a man who spent his entire life living in the so-called rarefied existence of Hollywood, but living a life, or several lives, or three or four lifetimes, in a very short span of time. He was a movie producer. He was a mega-lomaniac. He was interested in airplanes; you know, I have a love affair with airplanes ad nauseam, as did Hughes. And also he became completely reclusive and existed in kind of an inner world. And he was, at one point in his life, for several decades, the most gregarious person, and then the following several decades, the most infamously reclusive personality that's ever been talked about in American twentieth-century history. I just find that very fascinating. What drove him to the seclusion? What drove him into the rooms with the curtains drawn? It's a very interesting subject.

SISKEL: Do you think it was a physical problem or a mental problem?

SPIELBERG: I don't know. I don't know. I am exploring this the way everybody else is. I'm just in the middle of exploring Howard Hughes. So I'll be much more articulate about this a year from now.

SISKEL: What about a film that you might do next?

SPIELBERG: Several things I am thinking about, but nothing I am willing to talk about yet, only because when I tend to talk about things I kind of talk myself out of them, which is a big danger.

SISKEL: There was a film you were talking about doing with your sister.

SPIELBERG: Yeah, that's still on a burner.

SISKEL: What's that about?

SPIELBERG: It's just about a relationship. It's about a brother and sister growing up and it's really about when a brother and sister reunite after many years of estrangement and try to make up those lost years in their forties—the years they lost in their twenties.

SISKEL: Now, you focus on their making up, and you have right now sort of a smile on your face, and I almost think it would be a sweet film.

SPIELBERG: Yeah. I think it's a bittersweet film. It's probably the closest my sister and I both have come to talking much about each other and then making that public, which is always embarrassing.

SISKEL: But we've talked to directors like Martin Scorsese, and you know that if he were making that story he'd probably focus on the split.

SPIELBERG: Mm-hmm.

SISKEL: You'd focus, I have a feeling, more on the healing.

SPIELBERG: Yeah. This one's all about the healing. But also, you know, Marty is completely fluid about, and fluent in making movies about, who he is and his old neighborhood, his old haunts, his old friends. Marty is a truly personal American film-maker. And I've often taken the approach from my filmmaking that I am the audience. Lucky enough to have been given a camera at an early age and allowed to make movies for myself and, therefore, my friends sitting in the dark. So I've made movies that are bigger than life and movies that haven't hap-pened to me, but stories that I wish would happen to me and

characters I wish I could be more like. And I think that's where
we differ. Marty makes movies about characters he knows.

SISKEL: What director would you like to be like? Instantly! (Snaps
his finger.)

SPIELBERG: Victor Fleming. I mean, you asked the question:
"Instantly." Yes, because of his eclectic choices in his career and
the kinds of movies he made. I like Victor Fleming because he
was a hired hand. And I love the idea of not being an independent filmmaker. I've liked working within the system. And I've
admired a lot of the older directors who were sort of "directors
for hire." Like Victor Fleming was in a contract all those years to
Metro and Selznick and Mayer.

SISKEL: And the pictures of his that you would say, "Boy, I wish I
could have made that"?

SPIELBERG: Well, he made *Captains Courageous*. And you know, his
most famous films: *Wizard of Oz* and *Gone with the Wind. A
Guy Named Joe,* which I recently sort of reworked [as *Always*].

SISKEL: Now, here's a guy who turned himself over, as you said, and
his talents were in the service of filmmaking. You, instead, have
built your own empire, producing the films of others. I've often
wondered, why get involved with all of this stuff?

SPIELBERG: Well, I don't know. It's sort of just the whole machine of
making movies. It just swallows you whole, and it never regurgi-
tates you. You sort of sit in this fetid stomach of the process of
making and producing and engineering and creating movies.
And I've always liked to be kept busy. And when I knew I
wasn't going to be directing every eighteen months, I wanted
to fill up my time and be a producer and make the kind of movies that I'd like to see—even perhaps that I didn't want to actually direct but would certainly like to see as an audience. I got
involved with producing over the years that way. I also got involved with producing for an entirely different philosophy. It
was helping me get other filmmakers started, like Bob Zemeckis
and a number of young directors. I was successful and studios

were turning to me saying, "What do you have for us?" And I couldn't direct films for everybody, but I could produce films and I could allow these filmmakers to cut their teeth and get out there for the first time.

SISKEL: A long time ago you once told me, speaking of George Lucas, "Someday we'll all be working for George." But it's more likely, I think, that someday everyone will be working for you!

SPIELBERG: Well, I don't know. As a producer? No, not really. Because I'm not really interested. If that were true, I'd be running a studio by now.

SISKEL: You've had the offers?

SPIELBERG: Oh, yeah! Yes, many times, to really run a movie studio and make eighteen to twenty-five films a year! And I just don't want to do that, because how do you be attentive to eighteen to twenty-five movies a year? It's a business and sometimes you have to make movies you don't want to make to fill the bill. And that's a terrible way to get through your "creative" life, anyway.

SISKEL: In the nineties then, you're going to continue as a producer.

SPIELBERG: But in the late eighties I really haven't functioned as such. I haven't really produced the movies that sometimes bear my name. The company—Amblin Entertainment—the structure—Kathleen Kennedy, Frank Marshall [subsequent to this interview Marshall left the company]—they produce or executive produce the movies, and I pretty much decided several years ago to just direct. That's why I was able to make *Last Crusade* and *Always* and have them both released in the same calendar year, simply because I didn't produce two years before that and now I am not producing after that. Producing is a hard job for a director to do, because it presumes that my presence on a production is very intimidating to a filmmaker whose job it is to make the film, not to listen to my ideas. Because he has a personal vision; I have a personal vision. I often hire directors that don't share the same personal vision I have, so our visions would therefore clash if I ever really got involved as a producer.

And I found it safer and more attractive to other filmmakers to sort of get out of that area of the business and let them make their movies. I've gotten reinvolved if they've come to me—not me coming to them—and said, "Do you want to look at my rough cut?" Great, fantastic. "Any advice?" Sure, I'll give them advice. But if they don't ask, I don't offer.

SISKEL: Just out of curiosity, what advice did you give Bob Zemeckis on the first *Back to The Future* film? Anything big?

SPIELBERG: I don't know about the first *Back to The Future* film, but his first film with me was *I Wanna Hold Your Hand,* and I think the only advice we gave Bob was, "Wear comfortable shoes to work!" Because Bob had made a number of student films, and I just knew that he was ready. You can just tell when the egg is cracked and the hatchling is about to spring out. Bob was ready. Bob was ready years before he even made his first film, *Field of Honor,* at USC. I think my talent is being able to recognize who's ready to hatch and trying to get them to do an interesting film. And I don't do that all the time, but occasionally I've seen short films and found people. *Amazing Stories* is an example of that. *Amazing Stories* gave the opportunity for a lot of film students to direct professionally for the first time, as I had been given that opportunity when I first got started in the industry at twenty-one years old. A guy named Sid Sheinberg saw a short film of mine and hired me. I am just trying to pass the torch.

SISKEL: And you don't feel that all that effort takes away from you as a director?

SPIELBERG: It does. But one of the reasons I don't do that any more to that extent is because ideas that I liked to put in my own movies I used to share with others, and they were going into their films and not into my films!

SISKEL: Martin Scorsese said that you have in effect created a whole new genre of film, which is the spectacular entertainment. What is it like to walk around thinking, "I made *E. T.* I made it!"?

SPIELBERG: The big joy of course, is not so much thinking about,

"Gee, I made *E. T.*" It's when someone sees it for the first time, preferably a child, and really has an interesting reaction to it. When I go around beaming with pride is when someone who hasn't seen *E. T.* before sees it for the first time. Some Soviet circus performers came over to me at the interval at the Moscow Circus when it was in Los Angeles, and they had—certainly bootlegged—seen *E. T.* in the Soviet Union very, very recently. They were all in their fifties and sixties, these people who surrounded me. And they were pouring forth about *E. T.* as if they had been ten years old yesterday. That was one of the biggest thrills. That's what makes me think back to '82 saying, "God, I was lucky to have been able to be the one to make that movie."

SISKEL: Has your son seen it?

SPIELBERG: Yeah, he has. Yeah, several times.

SISKEL: What was that like the first time?

SPIELBERG: The first time . . . He saw it very young. He saw it when he was about two and a half. He was frightened in the first twenty minutes.

SISKEL: Same with my oldest daughter.

SPIELBERG: He was terrified. E.T.—he didn't know what an E.T. was. He didn't know whether E.T. was to be trusted. He didn't know whether E.T. was going to bring some sort of shadows of harm to the child in the bedroom. But once the Reese's Pieces came out and once E.T. began to trust him and he began to trust E.T., you know, Max completely became a prisoner of the experience and wanted to see it again when it was over with, which was wonderful. But now he prefers the cartoons. Now when I say, "Do you want to see *E. T.* again?" he says, "No, I want to see *Little Mermaid.*" So it's different. It's different every year.

SISKEL: How did you show him the film? Normally you would just slip in a cassette. I have a feeling you showed it to him in a screening room.

SPIELBERG: In perfect projection with perfect sound, 1.66 aspect ratio . . . Of course! I wouldn't let him see it on video.

SISKEL: Because . . .

SPIELBERG: Because there's an experience about sitting in a room, albeit maybe alone years after the film had its theatrical run. But seeing a large image, direct light through the celluloid, projecting like a slide show in movement against a screen with good sound and the smell of popcorn. It's exciting. It's theatrical. It's showmanship. Movies are showmanship. When movies go onto videotape, I love the idea that people still see our films in all different forms, but the showmanship is missing once you look at a movie at home.

SISKEL: It's not the same.

SPIELBERG: It's not the same.

SISKEL: Even in an intimate film, it's not the same.

SPIELBERG: No, it's not the same. It'll never be the same. And it's not the same really, sitting in a motion picture theater alone. It only really works for me—I am speaking personally—when I am in a movie theater filled with people who are all having subjective experiences, but with the same inspiration coming from that particular experience. They're being inspired. They're having personal experiences but they're all reacting, and that's why I am in this business. I am not really in this business to make movies that go directly onto videocassette and directly into the home.

SISKEL: Some people are suggesting this will be the very near future, which is that there will be direct projection in the home.

SPIELBERG: There will be, yes. There will be because they'll be made-for-home movies, the same way there's made-for-television movies. A lot of movies in the future will be made high definition, bypassing film and the process of the chemicals in film, and right onto cassette, right into an HDTV receiver. And it's going to look good, I guess, but it's not going to be film. It's not going to be grainy. It's not going to have a tactile vibration to it. Hopefully it's just going to be good storytelling by a different process.

SISKEL: And do you think the audience today really knows the difference? Or will know the difference in the nineties?

SPIELBERG: I think so. I think we always underestimate the audience, and I think that we always assume that the audience doesn't notice the small things. But you should see the kinds of letters I read from motion picture fans who catch the smallest mistake or notice the smallest touch that I don't think anybody would ever catch, that I just selfishly did for myself and put in the movie. It's amazing what people find when they see a film *once*! And maybe the reason audiences are so smart today is that television commercials and perhaps even music videos are quickening the mind, quickening the reaction time between a perceived image and how it's analyzed and how it comes in through your heart. And these kids can just process all this information faster than ever before in the history of media.

SISKEL: You seem to be saying that people are more visually literate.

SPIELBERG: They are. They're more visually literate, and they're also more hip about what you're trying to say. You know, we sit in story meetings saying, "Are they going to get it? Should we go back four scenes and lay some connective tissue, lay some pipe so it'll make sense to them, so the character will pay off?" They get it the first time. After a sneak preview I wind up taking out a lot of the gantry that supports the story when the audience is so far ahead of the movie. If they're too far ahead of the movie, then they're bored.

SISKEL: Can you give an example from one of your films, where you cut stuff out?

SPIELBERG: I took a lot of stuff out of *Close Encounters,* maybe not enough, but a lot of stuff in terms of the mountain. For some people who think that Richard was a little bit too obsessed with the shaving cream and the mashed potatoes, there were many more scenes involving the images of Devils Tower, Wyoming.

SISKEL: What else did he build it out of, for fans of that film?

SPIELBERG: Oh, he built it out of everything! He did a lot of thumb-nail sketching on matchbook covers; he saw his shadows on the wall at night just from moonlight coming in, projecting images of clothes hung over chair backs against the wall. There were a lot of different clues, and the audience didn't need it. They knew exactly where the story was going.

SISKEL: I must tell you, Martin Scorsese disagrees with you. He be-lieves that audiences are not as literate, and in particular film-makers are not as literate. That they don't have the training, the classical school training, to understand why you do certain spe-cific shots.

SPIELBERG: Yeah, sure. But that's two different things. That's film-makers and audience. Those are two different things.

SISKEL: Okay, let's talk about filmmakers. How literate are they?

SPIELBERG: I don't know. In the old days you didn't have to be that literate because there were great writers: F. Scott Fitzgerald and great novelists and short story writers working in the medium of motion pictures. Great playwrights then.

SISKEL: I think that he means visually literate.

SPIELBERG: Is he talking about the audience or the filmmakers today?

SISKEL: No, the director. He was also talking about the audience. He doesn't think that they can read films very well. He says that in effect, you give the audience a surfeit of riches that they don't even appreciate.

SPIELBERG: Well, there's no such thing, for me anyway, as a visually illiterate filmmaker. If they can capture something that never existed before, they're not handicapped. Just the whole Thomas Edison process of projecting shadows on the screen makes any-one behind the camera, no matter how befuddled, literate visually.

SISKEL: You are really the ultimate fan. I really believe it.

SPIELBERG: Yeah, I'm a big fan, I'm a big fan.

SISKEL: To say what you just said, which is that a director cannot be anything but magical . . .

SPIELBERG: Yeah, he can't be. Even if they have no training and they've never directed anything in their lives, something will happen when the camera is turned on. And something that director says, or some mistake he makes is going to be interesting.

SISKEL: Did you see the movie, *She's Out of Control?*

SPIELBERG: No. [Laughs]

SISKEL: [Laughs] Let me challenge you with that film!

SPIELBERG: Okay.

SISKEL: That's the one that made me want to resign after I saw it. It's so devoid of energy and all that.

SPIELBERG: A lot of people wish you would resign! [Laughs] A lot of people wish that film critics would be a whole different animal.

SISKEL: All right, let's talk about that. What would you prefer the future to be in film criticism?

SPIELBERG: You couldn't do it because you have a very important commercial show and it would be very hard for you with sound bites and being on the air, but if you could devote half an hour to one film, as opposed to a half an hour to four films, that would be really interesting. Nobody's ever done that before. And even if you devoted half an hour to a film that you and Roger didn't like, it would inspire a lot of other film clips from other films in your conversation with each other about why you didn't like it. I mean, I am interested in analysis, and sometimes it's really hard when you're juggling three, four, five films for twenty-two, twenty-three minutes. You know, minus commercials, not a lot of time to express yourselves. I've seen you guys overjoyed with a movie. I've seen you guys dying to get out all this wonderful feeling that the film gave you, and you don't have the time to do it. I guess what I would just say is, "More time." Longer reviews in newspapers, more writing. And less backbiting! Less, "Let's be clever with the negative, because it will make us look real good." I am talking about everybody, you know.

SISKEL: Yeah. I don't feel guilty on that.

SPIELBERG: The twisting of the sentence, you know, and the glibness or the hunger to go beyond criticizing and go into, I guess, a kind of personal meanness. Which I'm not accusing you guys of, I'm just saying there's an overall tendency in a lot of criticism today to really just get personal and get mean and kind of avoid the film and just make little personal attacks. I'd like to see that become a little less.

SISKEL: What can you say to the audience of the future? You just talked about a change in critics. We're going to let you play God in the next few questions.

SPIELBERG: Not to change the critics, but just the approach.

SISKEL: In the approach that they have. All right, let's make you God and say, talk about the audience in the same way. What would you like the audience to do in the future?

SPIELBERG: Well, you know, they've been doing pretty good up till now. Except they talk too much in the theaters! Have you ever sat in a theater where you're trying to follow the story and people were talking because someone who's not following the story is asking their friend to explain it to them? And they explain not only the story but where they're going to have supper after the film is over. I guess that's part of the experience, that's perhaps even part of the joy of moviegoing, that it's live: It's not your living room. You can't control strangers. You've got to sit there, you've got to be civilized, you've got to try to focus because there are sometimes many distractions that keep you from focusing. I don't know if you can change any of that stuff. I'd kind of like movie theaters to have little holes in the arms so you can put your Coca-Colas in there and stuff for your soft drinks and put your soft drinks in the hole. So my problem in going to a lot of movies, which I do, is I wind up with concession on my feet and I have to change my socks when I get back home!

SISKEL: The AMC theater chain does have it.

SPIELBERG: They do, in Century City. They do have it. I'd like to see that everywhere. That's nice. I am being a little bit glib here. What I am trying to say is, once the doors open and people run into a movie theater, as far as I am concerned really anything can happen. And not only is the film often the experience, but sometimes the reaction is the experience. That's why I always encourage people when they're seeing my movies, "Can you please not see them at home? Can you please maybe see them with an audience? Not to bias your opinion, but to share the experience that I've worked so hard to give everybody." To see *Indiana Jones and the Last Crusade* alone isn't as much fun as seeing it with an audience.

SISKEL: And of course, you've timed the film in editing, I would assume, for an audience.

SPIELBERG: Sometimes if we know we're going to get a laugh, a big laugh. I'll give you a perfect example. When we previewed *Raiders of the Lost Ark* and the swordsman goes at Indy with the sword and then Indy pulls the gun and shoots him, the reaction was not only big, it was sustained; it lasted a long time. And after the preview, I just added frames after that—I guess on stage, in theater, they say, "Hold for laughs"—just so we weren't so quick to get back into the story, to give the audience a chance to savor it, talk about it among themselves and then the story would reconvene, would continue. It wasn't a lot I added, but it was enough to let it kind of calm down. That's why previews are very helpful.

SISKEL: A second? Two seconds?

SPIELBERG: No, not even that. Maybe a second, maybe about 36 frames. But it was just enough! You know, it's interesting about movies. It's an art, it's not a science. It is a matter of what makes a scene sometimes work; I am talking about some kind of an action scene. Usually an action scene working or not working is often due to trims, tiny frames taken off or tiny frames added. It's all timing. And I think editors, film editors, are really unsung heroes in the cinema because of what they do in creating a kind of rhythm, even beyond what the director shoots. And even if the director is a major collaborator in the editing room, the editor is also a director when he's alone in the unventilated dark rooms with your movie, which then becomes sort of a shared experience. And those little cuts are crucial. I don't think people realize that.

SISKEL: You've been credited with creating a genre of the big, spectacular film. You have helped revive the animated film by executive producing *Roger Rabbit*. What can you do for the musical? Talk about what has to happen for you to revive the musical in the nineties.

SPIELBERG: The thing about reviving anything is that the seventies and the eighties were short-order decades. The nineties might be an even shorter-order decade, where the attention span of people for one subject doesn't last as long as it did in the seventies. I mean, there was a great appetite for space movies after *Star Wars* a lot longer than there have been for other flash-in-the-pan genres. People are really more eclectic today in terms of their taste. I believe audiences are. They want a little sampling of that, a little sampling of this, a comedy, a drama, a mystery, a love story. It's a bit of a cornucopia that seems to be more appetizing today. That's just my opinion. It seems that a wonderful musical could be made and there would be some imitations of the success, if the musical were to be successful. It doesn't necessarily guarantee that there's going to be a revival of the musical genre the way the war years needed the musical as a kind of an uplift—a national uplift.

SISKEL: What about somebody trying to recreate the [Arthur] Freed production unit at MGM?

SPIELBERG: Oh, it would be wonderful! Oh, are you kidding? It'd be great. The Freed unit was fantastic.

SISKEL: What's the problem? In other words, the classic perception

is that the audiences will not stand still for someone stopping
and starting to sing.

SPIELBERG: I am not sure if the audiences wouldn't prefer that to the
two-and-a-half-hour libretto. I am not quite certain yet if the
audience is ready for the light opera, the operetta, the *Phantom
of the Opera* and other things—*Jesus Christ Superstar* was
sort of opera from beginning to end. I am not quite sure if an
audience is ready for that as much as they are ready for a little
dialogue, a little music, a little dialogue, a few songs, a little
dialogue, a few songs, à la *West Side Story.* More recently in the
success category, *Grease,* whether you liked it or not, was an
old-fashioned musical revival. One of my favorite movies of all
time is *Singing in the Rain,* which tells a wonderful story that
didn't really need music, which is a nice kind of litmus test for
whether you should make a musical or not. If the book is strong
enough not to need music, maybe that would be a wonderful
musical.

SISKEL: And what about you? You have not attempted a musical.
Would you have any interest?

SPIELBERG: I've been looking to do one. I have a great appetite to
do a musical. A lot of my movies have had musical numbers in
them. I am a frustrated Busby Berkeley in that way, or a frustrated Stanley Donen. I'd very much like to work in that genre.

SISKEL: And you know this much about your power. If you do it,
even if you announce it all around this town, they're going to
start pulling the properties out of the drawers, right?

SPIELBERG: Well, it didn't happen when we announced *Peter Pan* as
a musical a number of years ago. No one was pulling properties
out of the drawer. But right now, I can tell you for a fact, studios
are looking for musicals. Almost every studio has musicals in
development right now. And we have a couple of things we're
playing with a little bit. I don't want to be too specific, but
they're musicals. It'd be wonderful to bring it back for a while,

anyway, as long as the audience would accept them, as good as they are.

SISKEL: What about *Peter Pan?*

SPIELBERG: I decided not to make *Peter Pan* really when Max was born, and I guess it was just bad timing. *Peter Pan* came at a time when I had my first child and I didn't want to go to London and have seven kids on wires in front of blue screens swinging around. I wanted to be home as a dad, not a surrogate dad. And I had made a lot of films with young people and I loved the experience and now I had something to really take personally. And so *Peter Pan* came at a very unfortunate time for the two of us.

SISKEL: Can you do it now?

SPIELBERG: Yeah, perhaps. But there's other kinds of musicals that I think I am a bit more interested in. [Subsequent to this interview Spielberg decided to make his *Peter Pan* film after all.]

SISKEL: What you seem to be telling me, and you've said it now twice, is with the birth of your child, and with the cleaning out of your drawer of adolescent fantasies, we're going to get a more adult cinema from Steven Spielberg in the nineties.

SPIELBERG: I don't know if it will be so much more adult. It will certainly appeal more to the people I grew up with: those I am growing old along with; all of us together that were kids when we saw *Star Wars*. We were kids when George made *Star Wars* and when I made *Jaws* and *Close Encounters*. We were kids then. And the generation of filmgoers that liked those movies is growing up right along with us. So hopefully the films that we make that might be perceived as being adult films will still be for the generation that enjoyed the films in the late sixties and early seventies.

SISKEL: Now, *Always* fits into that mode. You're forty-two now, and *Always* is a story about a man of forty-two, isn't it?

SPIELBERG: Yeah, sure, and my alter ego, Richard [Dreyfuss]. You know, we've done three films together now.

Robert Duvall in *THX 1138*, directed by George Lucas.

George Lucas directs *American Graffiti*.

George Lucas directs *Star Wars* with Harrison Ford.

Lucas believes that his work as a film-maker is best represented by his pace and editorial style. As an example, he mentions this sequence: "a very odd little sequence in *Star Wars*, where they escape from the Death Star and they're shooting the TIE Fighters . . . and they're in their gun ports."

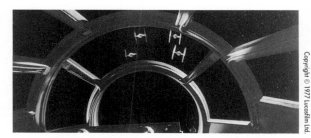

Steven Spielberg describes his "master image," the one frame that might summarize his style: "I think it's the little boy in *Close Encounters* opening the door and standing in that beautiful yet awful light, just like fire coming through the doorway. He's very small, and it's a very large door, and there's a lot of promise or danger outside that door."

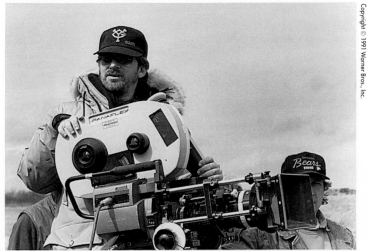

E.T. says goodbye to Elliot (Henry Thomas) before returning "home," in *E.T.—The Extra-Terrestrial* directed by Steven Spielberg.

Steven Spielberg directs.

Robert De Niro as Jake La Motta in *Raging Bull*. Martin Scorsese describes his "master image," summing up his style as a filmmaker, as the opening title shot from *Raging Bull*, which was not available for publication: "The sense of desolation, the sense of loneliness and that sense of that ring being in a way not different from the kitchen or the bedroom or the living room or the street."

Martin Scorsese directs.

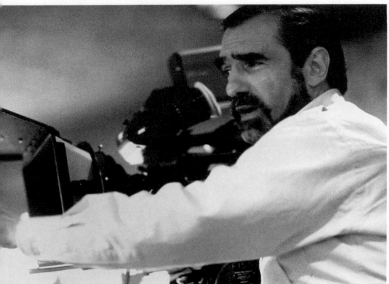

Harvey Keitel is seriously injured in a shootout in *Mean Streets*, directed by Martin Scorsese.

Cybill Shepherd and Robert De Niro in *Taxi Driver*, directed by Martin Scorsese.

SISKEL: You've talked about the aspirations of kids in your films to have a pet, an E.T.; to see a creature from another planet—*Close Encounters;* to survive a shark. What do forty-two-year-olds have fantasies about?

SPIELBERG: Well, forty-two-year-olds dream about spaceships, shark survival, fedora-hat-and-leather-jacket escapades across the globe. You know, forty-two years old, eighty-two years old, it doesn't matter what age you are: The child is still alive inside of you even if you dwarf it just by sheer neglect. And I think in a way it's irresponsible to neglect the child in each of us. And I know that's become a timeworn seventies, eighties cliché, but it still holds true. I hope I'm never accused of making "adult movies."

SISKEL: Because?

SPIELBERG: But I can't help the movies I make, you have to understand that. I don't sit down and plan my career like NASA plans the next shuttle launch. I don't sit down and say, "I think this would be good for me to do next because I haven't done it before." I'm really reactive and pretty emotional about the kind of things that I decide to do, whether it's something that comes past my face or something that I've had on my mind for a couple of years, or an idea that drops out of the sky and hits me. I don't say, "I can't do that, it's too much like this." I've been accused and rightly so in a way, of kind of wolfing down some of my own established genres. You know, people don't always like you very much for stealing from yourself. And yet I never really thought, "Gee, it's bad to steal from myself, maybe I shouldn't have done that in this movie, which reminds people of a film made eight years ago." For me, that goes to show that I don't give a lot of thought to that. I am just very reactive about the films, you know.

SISKEL: And later on, critics will look at you and say, "A body of work," because . . .

SPIELBERG: And I'll say they're right! I'll say, "Oh yeah, I did do that!" But at the time when I chose that particular movie it wasn't on my mind.

SISKEL: I want to ask a question again, because I don't know if you're giving me a really good answer.

SPIELBERG: Okay.

SISKEL: And that is, "What do forty-two-year-olds fantasize about?" Because I have a feeling that it is not creatures from another planet.

SPIELBERG: Well, the one thing we all have in common is a forty-two-year-old fantasizes about excitement and emotions whether they're uplifting or they're going to put your feelings down. It's the same as a child or a much older person.

SISKEL: I'm going to push you even more.

SPIELBERG: Okay, go ahead.

SISKEL: Obviously, I suppose, I'm talking about my own fantasies, but I would have thought that you would have said, "women." Or "men" for women.

SPIELBERG: I was giving you broader categories than simply men-women stories.

SISKEL: All right, but you have portrayed people that either want to be married or have been married for a while; this would be an obvious subject matter. And you always had a little bit of that going on. What about the ultimate sexual encounter, a truly "close encounter"?

SPIELBERG: *Moi,* to film that? [Laughs] I've always been embarrassed by screen sexuality. It's always embarrassed me. It's embarrassed me because it hasn't often been done real well, and when it has been done it's been no different than the last couple of sexual encounters in other movies. And one of the most original sexual encounters was one of the most honest, which was Nick Roeg's *Don't Look Now.* There haven't been a lot of *Don't Look Now*s since *Don't Look Now.* And I also find that movies tend to stop for love scenes; that what is said between the people in daylight is often much more poignant and emotional and sensually sug-

gestive than the arbitrary cutaway with the backlight coming
through the window and the rolling in the hay. To me there have
been very few films where that's important, and I personally
haven't really been attracted to that kind of film.

SISKEL: What about the sexuality of Howard Hughes? I would think
that would be very much a part of his life, both wanting to
touch, dating like crazy, and then not wanting to be touched.

SPIELBERG: Yeah, well, like I said before, I will come to know
Howard Hughes a lot more in the future than I do right now. But
there was quite a labyrinth in his mind and he is more complicated than being able to say that he was very overtly sexual to
women, and then all of a sudden using his eyes more than anything else, or his imagination. He's one of the most complicated
American business figures.

SISKEL: We've talked about what audiences can do in the nineties,
what critics can do in the nineties. What about film companies?
If you were king out here, and you are a prince at least, what
would you do? What do you say to the executives? Do you ever
give them advice? What would you like to see changed?

SPIELBERG: Well, "change," I don't know. I guess I would like to see
executives realize that they are sitting on a treasure chest of film
history right in their own vaults. And as these films sit in their
vaults they rot, they fade, they shrink; I'm talking about the
negatives now. I think I'd like to say to the executives something I've been saying all along, that they've got to spend more
time preserving their assets and "saving their assets," so to
speak. Going back into the vaults and picking great films to
preserve. And then to exhibit! I'd love to see more revival
houses. I'd love to see more old films shown in movie theaters,
not just at home.

SISKEL: Talk about the condition of your films. What are you doing
to preserve your films?

SPIELBERG: The first thing I do, which is in all in my contracts, I
make black and white separations so I can recombine the colors

later in the future to get wonderful results when my colors fade and I want to strike a new print of, let's say, *Sugarland Express*. They're just attended to, they're preserved, they're periodically checked, and I'm real concerned about that.

SISKEL: What does that cost the studio, to give you that clause on a film?

SPIELBERG: It costs them hardly anything at all, I guess, to give me that clause. I've made, what, eleven films? Let's say the films were in terrible condition. To restore eleven pictures would probably cost the studio upwards of about half a million to a million dollars.

SISKEL: So, $50,000 a picture?

SPIELBERG: Yeah, something like that, if they really need preservation. My films don't, but I'm talking about if I was this old codger sitting here and I made all these great films back in the thirties. It would cost a little bit more when they're worse for wear.

SISKEL: That doesn't seem like much of a price for these companies to pay.

SPIELBERG: No, it doesn't. And actually for some films it's less than that. In some films you can preserve a film for three or four thousand dollars.

SISKEL: I think you told Roger and me that *Jaws* was not in good shape.

SPIELBERG: It's in terrible shape. And we have been going all over the world looking for good prints that might have been misplaced when the film was first exhibited in Europe, let's say in 1975. We've been looking for good prints around. We haven't really found any; we're working on the negative now to try to strike some good prints off of the negative, which also isn't in great shape.

SISKEL: What happened?

SPIELBERG: Just bad storage. Bad preservation techniques, that's all there is to it. The Egyptians knew how to preserve their people three thousand years ago. We don't know how to preserve our

film in the nineties! And there are people who know how to do
it. It's just going to take money and a commitment on the part of
the owners, the corporations, to really want to save their films.

SISKEL: Scorsese said he think's it's in their interest, and all you have
to do is make them aware it's in their financial interest.

SPIELBERG: Yes, yes, exactly.

SISKEL: He said you don't need what I suggested, let's say, a ten-cent
tax on every ticket.

SPIELBERG: No, not at all.

SISKEL: The public shouldn't have to pay for it?

SPIELBERG: No! The public shouldn't pay a cent for the film companies, the copyright holders to protect their assets, as I said
before. They have a responsibility certainly to their own
shareholders and to their own partners. They also have a responsibility to the audiences. This is the entertainment industry; we make movies to entertain people. And there's so much
foresight now about what happens, what's the life span of a
movie. The life span of a movie is a lot longer than it ever has
been in history because of television, because of videotape
players, and other future technologies. But basically I'm still
interested in showmanship and exhibition. And I'm real concerned that even though they say, "Don't worry, our films are
preserved on videotape," well, videotape also falls apart! They
say, "Don't worry, we're preserved on disc." Well, discs can get
ruined. I think they've got to go back to the negative—which is
just short of the inspiration, which is always a filmmaker—and
take those little nuggets and treat them like antiquities. Treat
them the way people run around spending thousands of millions
of dollars buying French Impressionism. Let's treat our films like
they're works of art and not just commodities to be rolled off
and rolled off and rolled off until someday in the future they'll
be able to cut off the heads of the actors from the nineties and
put on the heads of the popular actors from the twenty-first
century!

SISKEL: You referred to the inspiration being the filmmaker, yet the

THE FUTURE OF THE MOVIES

filmmaker doesn't hold the copyright. Are you in favor of this so-called "moral rights legislation"? Can you tell us what it is? I know you're in favor of it.

SPIELBERG: Jeez! Okay, yes, I completely recognize that the corporations hold the copyright, but I think the artists have a kind of moral copyright that happens at the point of conception. When John Huston made *The Treasure of the Sierra Madre,* and he wrote and he directed it—based on a book, I believe, or a story—that became as much his film morally as it became Warner Brothers' film under the law. Now we move into the late twentieth century and all of a sudden technology shows us another way of exhibiting John Huston's films, which is by colorizing them. That's just the tip of the iceberg, but it's how this whole brouhaha began. In doing a black and white film, which is an artistic selection, the filmmaker had a choice. Huston was a powerful filmmaker when he made *The Treasure of the Sierra Madre.* He could have gone to the studio and said, "For a few dollars more, make it in color." He chose black and white. The same way the Academy of Motion Picture Arts and Sciences recognized black and white as distinguished from color by honoring black and white with an Oscar as well as color films with an Oscar, up to about twenty years ago. Ansel Adams would look pretty silly—a man who mastered the black and white form—with his black and white plates colored in. And I'm just saying that I'm for this: I'm for showing my children John Huston's movies—as one example—the way John Huston wanted his films to be made, not the way a corporation wanted to remake John Huston's movies. I want the Real McCoy shown to my kids.

SISKEL: The argument goes beyond colorization, though.

SPIELBERG: Yes, it does.

SISKEL: Because it would say that your films cannot be shown on television without your participating in any editing.

SPIELBERG: Sure, absolutely, because what happens often is they do

two things on television. They speed films up electronically so
they can get more commercials in. And sometimes they edit the
films almost arbitrarily to fit a time slot. I don't think a film
should be shown, except in its original version, ever! People
might say, "Well, we kind of like the abridged, digested version
of the film." If they really saw the original movie they probably
wouldn't. Now you can also make the argument that there are
some very bad films, so who cares about them? Well, I think
morally this has to cover all films, because who's to say what's
good or what's bad? It's very subjective. I guess the main thing
is that I believe that art and film go hand and hand. Films have
outgrown their days at the nickelodeon, and they're not just
concessions, and they're not like fast food really, and they're
not like vending machines. Time and again movies have been
acknowledged around the world as art. But they're not treated
as art. They're treated as concessions. I think that once a movie
is made and the studio pays for the movie and the film hits the
motion picture theater and starts to run, there should be a
freeze on that movie; nothing can be done to change or alter
that movie without the consent of the principal writer and the
principal director. They have to both consent—kind of a fail-safe
operation—for like a dollar in payment, to any network wanting to come in and shorten the film or colorize it or what have
you. And that should apply to all the arts.

SISKEL: We're talking about changes, if you were king. What about
changing film equipment? Is there an invention that you would
like to see happen in the nineties that would help you make
films better?

SPIELBERG: No, no. I think motion picture's a unique medium. Film
and cameras and everything we have right now is all we need. I
really believe that. It's all we need. Can you invent a new kind of
bat to hit a baseball further, without cheating? There are certain
forms in our culture, and sport has been there for a long time.
It doesn't need improvement. Football doesn't need a replay

judge; I think that's a real burden of technology on human errors and judgment calls, whether right or wrong. But films have a camera, we've got the lab to process the film, we've got the lights, we've got the sound. No, I think we've got all we need.

SISKEL: You don't strive to use the best high-speed film and the best cameras, I mean?

SPIELBERG: Sure, but you can't get any better than the cameras that they've made right now, I don't think, unless they find a new process. Unless we all start making Omnimax movies or Imax movies someday to compete against HDTV, which might happen. When HDTV really comes into this country it's going to take this country by force. First of all, people who can afford it will buy it, and later the sets will get cheaper and that's going to compete theatrically, because the pictures are going to be as clear almost, in your home, as 35-millimeter movies. And that's when we might have to start thinking about a different kind of formatting of the motion picture experience: larger theaters, bigger screens, first and foremost better stories. I mean technology is nothing, and the craft of making movies is nothing unless you've got a good story to tell. It all starts there; that's the beginning. And the end, often.

SISKEL: It would be a complete misreading of you then if someone does a retrospective of you at the end of the nineties, to say, "This is the guy who made the spectaculars," because that implies simply scale and size and shape. You're a storyteller, that's what you're saying.

SPIELBERG: Yeah, I think I am. I remember David Lean, before his American Film Institute Life Achievement Award, was just concerned that the people who selected the clips of all of his films wouldn't just dwell on a thousand extras in the background in *Lawrence of Arabia,* or the same number of extras in Red Square from *Doctor Zhivago.* He was hoping that the film clips would be about performance and story and intimacy and not

just the tapestry of his films. And I feel the same way, in that
sense.

SISKEL: How much time do you spend on story construction, before
you start storyboarding?

SPIELBERG: Story construction—that has to do with the development of the story and the screenplay. *Always*—but for very
personal reasons—took me ten years, to find the angle to tell the
story, the sort of approach to telling the story. I didn't quite
know how to make that movie for a decade, partially because I
wasn't, in 1980, grown up enough to make that movie! And I
had other things that I really wanted to make more than that
movie. But the storyboarding really only happens with me
when I'm making an action film or sequences with a lot of
special effects, where everybody needs to really know what's
happening, every department needs to really see a picture
worthy of a thousand words. And that's why I storyboard; I
storyboard for action, mainly. I've never storyboarded anything
having to do with two people in a room talking. *The Color
Purple* had no storyboards, *E.T.* had only a couple of storyboards involving flying across the moon and anything involving
a special effect. *Empire of the Sun* did have storyboards with
the crowd scenes, but had no storyboards with anything about
the boy story. So I've been very careful about that.

SISKEL: When you just said the phrase, "flying across the moon,"
where were you when you came up with that one?

SPIELBERG: I don't know where ideas come from in that sense. I
don't know, that was just an image that struck me. It was, I
guess, the cow jumping over the moon, when I was a child and I
heard the nursery rhyme. And instead of a cow it was a boy on a
bicycle with an extraterrestrial in the basket in front. And it was
just an image that I thought would be delicious for the movie.
And you know, it happened: I got the idea—I don't know
whether it was an early idea that was actually part of the screenplay or whether it was a later idea. I just called ILM, and I said,

"Can you do it so a boy can fly across the moon? Can you do that? Huh? Can you, can you?" I don't know when that idea happened, but it did happen.

SISKEL: Even your voice there, "Can you, can you, can you?"

SPIELBERG: Yeah, yeah.

SISKEL: That's like a little kid. You just again became a little kid. Now you're forty-two years old, are you going to "grow up" in the nineties?

SPIELBERG: I don't know. I'm not going to say, "I hope so." I'm not looking to grow up in the nineties, I'm not making a conscious effort to grow up in the nineties. I think I'm changing all the time, but I also think that I'm not going to know really who I am through my movies until I've made a lot more films, and can look back and say either, "I grew up" or "I never grew up." That's not my problem.

SISKEL: Then what is?

SPIELBERG: I don't have any problems in that regard. My problem is finding good stories from my own imagination. It's never been easy. Talk to producers on Broadway in the old days, "We've got to have a show. We've got to have a show." Pacing, you know, smoke coming out of their feet as they pace, hours in a hotel room trying to think of a show. It's the age-old problem: What do we do to entertain you next? What do we do to entertain ourselves next?

SISKEL: But see, even just now you come up with a great visual image—the smoke under the feet.

SPIELBERG: Yeah, I'm a Toon, Gene! I'm a Toon, okay? [Laughs]

SISKEL: Do you see movies looking or sounding different in the nineties? Again, HDTV is the buzz word.

SPIELBERG: Right, right. That's for home though, that's not movies.

SISKEL: And you talked about that in the theater. If we get HDTV then we may get even more spectacular films.

SPIELBERG: I don't know if you'll get more spectacular films, but you might get a much more environmental medium of presentation, like a screen that's five stories high, like Imax is today.

SISKEL: Right.

SPIELBERG: It's very hard to see an Imax movie though, because you can't cut, you can't edit on Imax. You can't do an action sequence like the truck chase in *Raiders* in Imax. Because you'd get a headache. The screen size is so large, when you'd change an image, it's jarring. The screen is so large, your eye has to scan everywhere quickly to see what the image is. MTV would not be good in the Imax process! But I'm sure that Hollywood and the scientists and the technicians will find a way to present something much more spectacular if HDTV in fact becomes competitive. We're talking down the road a piece.

SISKEL: You're going to get this question till you drop: the *E.T.* sequel.

SPIELBERG: Mm-hmm.

SISKEL: In the nineties?

SPIELBERG: No. Go further.

SISKEL: 2010?

SPIELBERG: No. [Laughs]

SISKEL: 2020?

SPIELBERG: Nope. [Laughs]

SISKEL: And just so people understand, when you say "no" you're saying "no" to probably hundreds of millions of dollars. You know that.

SPIELBERG: Yeah, yeah.

SISKEL: You could even fund film preservation and moral rights legislation by buying every senator in the United States!

SPIELBERG: [Laughs] I'll buy it with *Raiders of the Lost Ark*. I don't mind making a lot of those. I don't think I'll make any more after three. But I mean certainly I'm not against sequels, because we've been the producers of the three *Back to the Future* movies which really is like one story divided up into first, second, and third acts. And *Raiders* is not really a trilogy, but it's three adventures. But I would never make a sequel to *Close Encounters of the Third Kind,* because I liked the way the film ended, and I'm not curious about what happens next. And I would never make a sequel to *E.T.,* because I'm also not curious about what happens next. It ended. It was a wonderful love affair, and then it was over. And then Elliot went back to his life, and E.T. went back to his planet. There's no going back, there's nothing more to say. I said it all. But with *Raiders* I had an appetite, as George did, for more adventure, and I still have an appetite to make adventure movies. Not the *Raiders* type of film, but I still want to do adventure films in my career.

SISKEL: When you said E.T. went back to his life I think I know what Elliot's life might be like. He might grow up to be you, right?

SPIELBERG: Yeah, I always thought Elliot grew up to be a kind of modern-day Tom Swift, that he became a Tom Swift character.

SISKEL: What about E.T.'s life? What would this little guy do?

SPIELBERG: Oh, well, you know, E.T. went back. We wrote a book about this. William Kotzwinkle, a wonderful science fiction writer, wrote a book called *E.T. and the Green Planet.* It's really a story about E.T. going back to his planet, and we saw what his life was like back there.

SISKEL: And you wouldn't want to film that?

SPIELBERG: No, no. But there's an attraction at Universal Studios in Florida which is a trip to E.T.'s planet. I mean, if you're dying for the sequel, then the next best thing is to jump on a little bicycle in Florida at Universal Studios and take off and fly to his planet and see what it looks like with E.T.

SISKEL: And why spend your time on that?

SPIELBERG: I just think that there's something all so interesting about live performances. It's one step, for me, short of the legitimate theater, being able to sit with the park and recreation designer people and working up an *E.T.* attraction or a *Back to the Future* attraction that will play fifteen hours a day, seven days a week. That's exciting, that's like a movie that never closes. And that was exciting; a kind of immortality crept into the equation when they seduced me to be the consultant with the park and said, "You know, as long as the park is successful, E.T. will always play in the park." And I thought, "Wow!" It's kind of like *Cats* at the Winter Garden in New York, isn't it? He's playing and playing and playing. That was exciting!

SISKEL: And you say that, even though your movie obviously is one of the most rented, purchased films. You still feel that the park is immortality?

SPIELBERG: Oh, no, no, movies are certainly, all this stuff. I think we're all in it, in a way, for a kind of immortality, which is what artists do. Painters, architects, actors, actresses, writers, novels, it's all sort of based on that, isn't it?

SISKEL: Let's look on the dark side and let's say your life is cut short. Let's say you can't make any more films. What will you regret not having made? "I didn't do this."

SPIELBERG: I don't know. I don't have any regrets, which is kind of nice. I don't really have any regrets. There's a lot that I want to do. I mean, if I was really satisfied, I probably wouldn't be working anymore.

SISKEL: Right.

SPIELBERG: But I don't have an agenda to satisfy me. Every day is like new. Every day is one more step toward some kind of discovery. And I don't plan that far ahead for myself. I don't plan that far ahead, because if I do, I will make the movie in my mind, or I will make some kind of thing happen for me in my mind, and I'll live it in my mind, and then I won't want to make it. So only I get to share it, nobody else gets to see that movie, because I've just explored it too much.

SISKEL: Can you tell me one that you've played out in your mind?

SPIELBERG: *Peter Pan* was a movie I played out in my mind. I made that movie ten times in my head until I just didn't want to go to the floor to make it. There's been a number of things that I've thought about too much, and the movies that most satisfy me that I've made are the films that I didn't think about at all. The ones that I said, "That's great! I want to make that movie," and I make it that year. I don't wait three, four years to make it.

SISKEL: And what surprised you by the way it turned out, from the way it may have occurred to you so that you said "I didn't know it was going to look like this!"

SPIELBERG: They all do. You know, Gene, they all do. When I get involved in the process of scripting and then directing and cutting the whole thing, I never know how they're going to turn out until I see them cut for the first time. There's a very magical moment that happens, and I don't know if Marty and George have shared this same experience, but you walk into a screening room and your editor is about to present to you your own movie, seen by you for the first time. It's not even called a rough cut, it's called an assemblage. It's a frightening day of the year. It should only happen to you once a year if you make only one movie a year. It's a very frightening thing. And that's where you sit down and you try to be objective, but you either go with the movie and you're entertained by it or enlightened by it or disturbed by it, or you shut it out, and you have no reaction, which is the most dangerous thing to have happen to you, when you don't react to the first time you've seen something you've done. I've just pretty much found that's the scariest moment in the whole process for me. I have no control over it, and that's why I'm always surprised.

SISKEL: So you won't say as a filmmaker, "You know, I never made a Western?"

SPIELBERG: Well, I never wanted to make a Western. [Laughs]

SISKEL: "I never made a musical?"

SPIELBERG: I've made enough fragments of musicals in all my movies that if I cut them together it would kind of be like *Hellzapoppin.* Including *1941,* which should have been a musical.

SISKEL: I think you're right.

SPIELBERG: Yeah, yeah, that should have been a musical. That was a book—not a very strong book—but that was a book that could have stood about eleven songs. Hey, Gene, maybe I'll go back and remake that! [Laughs]

SISKEL: Well, you did give us the collectors' edition of *Close Encounters.*

SPIELBERG: With *Close Encounters,* I didn't really want to show the inside of the mother ship, but it was the only way I could get the money out of Columbia! Because they needed a real hook to be able to justify rereleasing the film, and I was dying to edit the movie. My big contribution to *Close Encounters of the Third Kind—Special Edition* was the editing and the fine tuning that I was denied the chance to carry out, because Columbia for financial reasons had to have the film mid-November in theaters in 1977. It was a big corporate crunch, and I got caught right in the middle of it. I tried to help them, and I rushed my film through post-production as quickly as we could get the effects done. And certainly I spent more time on the effects that I really should have spent in the editing room on the cut. And I got a chance to sort of reshape the movie; I added a few scenes that were in the original script I'd never shot, that I wished I had shot. And I'm really happy with the *Special Edition* up until Richard gets on the mother ship. The minute he gets on the mother ship I'm not happy with it, until the end.

SISKEL: It's like looking behind the curtain?

SPIELBERG: Yeah, yeah, exactly. The audience saw much more from the exterior of the mother ship than I showed them four years later, with the reissue of the *Special Edition.*

SISKEL: Which is why you don't want to show us E.T.'s life on his planet.

SPIELBERG: Yeah, because your imagination is better than mine, and the collective imagination is wonderful, and they will dream *E.T.* sequels from now until they get tired of thinking about that little squashy guy. And that's wonderful, knowing that people

THE FUTURE OF THE MOVIES

think of their own stories. But I don't want to think for them. I'd like to just be inspired by the first film, if they were, and take it from there.

SISKEL: We're talking about changing movies in the nineties. What would you like to do to all the theater owners? We've left them out. The theater owners. Most films, you know, are not shown with the light on the screen that you want to be there. Can you talk about that?

SPIELBERG: Well, I would certainly hope that theater owners take as much pride in exhibiting our films as we do in having made them.

SISKEL: You know they don't.

SPIELBERG: But if they did, then there would be an average of fifteen to seventeen foot-lamberts, which means the amount of light: a good, healthy amount of projection light onto the screen.

SISKEL: And what is there in an average theater, instead of fifteen to seventeen?

SPIELBERG: Six or seven, sometimes. Sometimes we actually have to anticipate where our films are being exhibited so we can put more light, in the lab, into our films, so when they show in theaters that customarily run films with very weak projector bulbs you get to see the image on the screen! Sometimes we time our movies specifically for theaters with low projection output.

SISKEL: Is that because they want to save on electricity?

SPIELBERG: No, just because they're not aware of it. And I'm not sure if it's a savings thing. It's just that they put the films on the racks and they press a button and they roll. Nobody checks the sound. I just wish there were theater managers that would check the sound rather than having someone in the theater come up and bang on the door, which I'm sure you know happens all the time: "It's too loud! We can't hear it! It's out of focus. It's framed up too high, you're cutting off the guy's eyes!" I wish there was the same kind of pride of exhibition, and that's the one thing I would wish on to the nineties, that theater owners take a personal pride. I was an exhibitor when I was twelve, thirteen, fourteen years old. I exhibited 16-millimeter movies for a charity in my dad's family room in Phoenix, Arizona. And I never made those movies. I never made *Davy Crockett* or *Toby Tyler* or any of the Disney films that were available to me to exhibit for this charity. But in watching the reaction of the kids getting off on the movies I felt as if I had made those films. And I know the satisfaction an exhibitor can have, and the pride, of showing a wonderful film in his theater in perfect conditions.

SISKEL: I've come up with an idea that I offered for free to the world, where I said, "Call it 'First-Class Cinemas.'" Charge 50 percent more—instead of seven bucks, $10.50! "But if we don't show you a film in perfect condition with perfect sound, you get your money back or a coupon for the next picture. But it's going to cost a lot to get those speakers balanced and everything, and we're going to have somebody *in* the auditorium at all times." What about an idea like that?

SPIELBERG: Well, we already have something like that. We don't have a rebate program. But we have something like that in that audiences are so savvy that when they see "70-millimeter" they know that that's probably going to be the National Theater, in Westwood, one of the best theaters in southern California. They pretty much know that 70-millimeter carries with it great sound, in focus, well-framed, and clean theaters. Because most of the 70-millimeter houses are quite extraordinary. Very well kept up houses. And there is a pride of exhibition in a lot of the "70" houses. And we did a study during *Star Wars* and *Close Encounters,* because we were really interested in whether "70" was getting more people in theaters than "35," and yes, it was; "70" was attracting the majority of the audience to the films that were being shown in 35 millimeter four blocks away—the same movie.

SISKEL: Then people must say, "What does it cost to get everything shown in '70'?"

SPIELBERG: It costs more. A big problem is you can only make a couple of prints a day. You know we're always late in getting our movies finished. And then they'd have to start printing "70's." And to print an order of something like 350 70-millimeter prints takes a long time, when you think about two to four prints a day, if they run all night.

SISKEL: And it costs how much more for a "70" print?

SPIELBERG: I don't know the exact figure; it's substantially more. But it's worth it, because audiences are attracted very much not only because it's 70-millimeter, but also because they know the sound's going to be fantastic. Because with 70-millimeter comes magnetic sound, which is much better than what you can get in 35-millimeter theaters.

SISKEL: So people should read the ads, and if they see a Spielberg film or anybody's . . .

SPIELBERG: Or let's say they see *The Hunt for Red October*. They see it in "70" and they see it down the block at "35." They'll probably go to the "70" theater, because they will just intuit that the presentation will be much better there.

SISKEL: One of the best things that a critic ever said about you was said by Vincent Canby of the *New York Times*. He called you "the poet of suburbia."

SPIELBERG: [Laughs]

SISKEL: I wish I had written that sentence. How does that fit for a description of you?

SPIELBERG: Well, because it was my roots, so to speak. I was raised in suburbia; it's all I know. I wasn't raised in a big city. I wasn't raised under the shadows of skyscrapers. I lived under the sky all through those formative years, from third grade right through high school. That's my knowledge of a kind of lifestyle.

SISKEL: And today?

SPIELBERG: I still live in suburbia, in a way. I live in a different kind of suburbia, but it still is. There are houses next door and across the street, and you can walk, and there are street lamps on the street and sidewalks, and it's very nice.

SISKEL: Could you make a city film?

SPIELBERG: No. Not as well as people like Marty or Brian [DePalma] or city-bred boys and girls. I don't think so.

SISKEL: You know you get people who like your work and want you to be a Scorsese.

SPIELBERG: Be somebody else! A lot of people like my work, and they say, "Now, can you be somebody different?" And I say, "What's wrong with me?" And they say, "We like all your films up till now, but you're starting to repeat yourself, and we're getting a little tired of this sweet stuff. Why don't you be somebody else and make a real dark movie? Show us your dark side!"

SISKEL: And in the nineties, they're not going to get it, right?

SPIELBERG: I haven't shown *myself* my dark side yet! How am I going to show it to anybody else? We've all got them, but we have to acknowledge them before we can make movies about them. No, we all do different things. I could never make *Raging Bull.* I don't think Marty could have made, let's say, *Close Encounters,* in the same way. He'd have made a wonderful and interesting *Close Encounters.* I don't think I would have made a wonderful or interesting *Raging Bull!* Marty likes primal life, he likes the primal scream. He's the best director of the primal scene in film history. The primal scream scares the stuff out of me, and I've been avoiding it all my life. And so I make movies that are a little bit above life, or below life, but not real life! Beyond real life. And those are the kinds of films that have always attracted me. So I wouldn't be good at making an eye-level movie, I think, even now when I'm forty-two. I don't think I would be any better at it now than I might have been ten years ago. But we'll see, who knows?

SISKEL: This came from Marty a long time ago. He told me about the concept of a "master image," which is that one frame from a picture that can summarize the film. The boy going over the moon in the bicycle. What about a master image—this is real tough. I start throwing out all your films, and you say, "Give me this one negative—let me hold this one!" What occurs to you?

SPIELBERG: That's the best and maybe the hardest question to answer, because it's kind of like saying, "Which of your four kids do like the most?" It's hard for a parent to answer that when they have a lot of children. I don't know. I'm not sure. You're asking the question and I feel obligated to give you an answer, so let me give you an answer even if I take it back in my sleep tonight, okay?

SISKEL: Fine!

SPIELBERG: I think it's the little boy in *Close Encounters* opening the door and standing in that beautiful yet awful light, just like fire coming through the doorway. And he's very small, and it's a very large door, and there's a lot of promise or danger outside that door. I think that might be an interesting image for me. That's the first thing that came to mind, anyway, when you asked the question. And that must mean something.

SISKEL: And what it means to you is basically a symbol of the human condition? That we're all boys or girls standing in front of a door at all times?

SPIELBERG: That we don't know what's out there, and yet we should discover what's out there. We should be afraid of not knowing. And we should take a step toward what we don't understand and what we don't know about and what scares us. And we should embrace what scares us. We shouldn't be self-destructive about it, but we should go toward that kind of proverbial light and see what's out there for us.

SISKEL: And we'll do that with you in the nineties. What would you like to see filmmakers as a group do more in the nineties?

SPIELBERG: As David Lean said at his tribute, we too often come out of the same hole and we should all be coming out of different holes more and more, especially because it seems to be harder and harder to find original stories. We should be working harder to find those original stories. But also, just talking film here for a second, I'd love to see directors not shoot so many closeups. I'd love to see directors start trusting the audience to be the film editor with their eyes, the way you are sometimes with a stage play, where the audience selects who they would choose to look at while a scene is being played, with two characters, four characters, six characters. There's so much cutting and so many closeups being shot today I think directly as an influence from television. That has carried over indelibly into motion pictures of the late twentieth century. And as a result, it's too easy for filmmakers. It's very easy to put somebody up against a wall and shoot a closeup, and they say the words and you go on to the next shot. But to stage a scene the way Mike Nichols does theater, and does films as well, and he does stage very beautiful wide shots—long continuous shots—I'd like to see some staging come back. It's a skill; you can learn how to do it. It's hard, it's much harder, getting two, three actors in a room and saying, "Okay, I'm going to shoot this kind of loose, and let's talk and move and figure out what the body language is, why we're this close to each other or this far apart," and start telling stories without the simple choker—the claustrophobic closeup which doesn't really show you enough, because you cut off the hands. Part of our expression is what we do with our hands and how our bodies are, and what position we're leaning in the chair, and it's all about that. And I just think it's one of the more negative influences television's had on this current generation of filmmakers.

SISKEL: As filmmakers get older, traditionally they have gone for the all-in-one shot. Jean Renoir. All-in-one, less and less cutting. Do you see that going on in your life as you get older?

SPIELBERG: I've always shot not tight, unless it's important. What pulled me into shooting closeups was when I shifted to the widescreen format. You know, 2.35 aspect ratio—Panavision, if you will. And it's hard to shoot in that aspect ratio. It's much easier to shoot in 1.66, or 1.33, which was the famous format for the musical numbers that you could see from head to toe of Fred Astaire and Gene Kelly dancing with Ginger Rogers and Cyd Charisse. And I kind of miss that, but I find in a lot of my movies that I do try to practice what I preach. I shoot close when I think there's a dramatic reason to be close, when it's going to better tell the story to be intimate with the person speaking. And then when it doesn't matter, when we're just moving the story forward, I don't often just say, "Get me a closeup," when it's not to make a point.

SISKEL: Let's, in a brief example, pick a scene from your film where you keep it wide. Talk me through a scene; let's take Indiana Jones, if you will.

SPIELBERG: We're not just talking about long sustained shots, but about keeping things so the audience has a chance to see what's happening in the frame. A very simple example that comes to mind is a kind of expository sequence in *Last Crusade,* where Brodie and Indy are sitting in a hotel room and Brodie's been hit over the head and he has an ice pack to his head and he's poring over the Grail diary, Sean Connery's Grail diary. It's pretty much just shot as two men sitting around a kind of coffee table discussing where they go next with the story. It was a wide two-shot with a slow camera move in and a slow camera move out with a couple of inserts in between. But it was very loose and casual and the audience had a chance to make their own choices of who they look at. Scorsese's certainly very good about the sustained master, and *Raging Bull* has some wonderful sequences, just people around the table talking, and you feel like you're also at the table. The audience is given the chance to be at the other end of the table. And they're also given the chance and perhaps the privilege of deciding who they look at. There are five people around the table; Marty's not doing five closeups, he's doing one master shot and the audience has to supply the closeups. They have to find who they're interested in watching, listening to, and then they become the film editor. I think that gives the audience credit and makes them participate in the movie more.

SISKEL: Psychologically, if you start flashing closeups, I believe that we blink almost and are pushed back in our theater seat,

whereas if you hold all in one and let us search the frame,
by definition our eye is up on the screen.

SPIELBERG: It's true, absolutely true. In *Jaws* there are some sustained
scenes when Richard Dreyfuss and Robert Shaw are talking
about their scars, they're comparing scars. Rather than break it
up into single, single, single, single, single, it played better with
these two men in just a two-shot for a long time as they compared every scar on their arm, leg, and everywhere else. And
comedy plays better in wider shots. Somehow it's funnier
seeing the whole person than just a part of the person, with
comedy especially. But in the old days of Howard Hawks and
His Girl Friday, they were like stage plays on film. Long sustained masters. One of the most famous that comes to mind is
the opening sequence in Preston Sturges's *Sullivan's Travels,*
where the film director comes in to pitch the movie producer a
tragedy he wants to make and they try to talk him out of it. It is
one shot brilliantly staged, brilliantly rehearsed by the actors—
must have been days of rehearsal—and spoken as fast as
Rosalind Russell and Cary Grant ever spoke their dialogues
in *His Girl Friday.*

SISKEL: What does it do for the audience to see them talking
together, rather than closeups cutting from one to the other?
Where does that place us?

SPIELBERG: It makes the audience feel that subconsciously someone
is not manipulating what they're watching, someone is not
intruding upon what they're watching by having a big finger
pointing, "Look at this, look at this now, look, look over here,
look over here, look, look, look." The audience isn't having
me in their faces saying, "Look, look, look, look, look." The
audience gets a chance to take a breath between action sequences. But we *are* saying, "Look, look, look, look, look"
if the shark ever worked! And I had to say, "Don't look, don't
look, don't look" so you could look over there so you don't see
what didn't work over there! Instead the audience gets to sit

there, and with the pressure off enjoy the presentation of these two characters really enjoying each other's stories and company and differences.

SISKEL: Of course, the ultimate manipulation is not having us feel manipulated, right?

SPIELBERG: Everything about movies is manipulative; when you walk into the theater you're buying a ticket to manipulation! And all this accusation about how manipulative we are—perhaps more specifically I am—is nonsense, because the whole process is manipulating something that wasn't, until you got into the

theater and then it is.

SISKEL: That's why we all go to the theater.

SPIELBERG: It's why we go to the movies.

SISKEL: What will the effect be of all people having cameras now and taking their pictures on vacation? Is this going to help visual literacy, or how is this going to affect the films of the nineties?

SPIELBERG: I'm not sure it's going to affect the films of the nineties at all, because I don't think that camcorders are really any different than the Kodak Brownie still cameras that my parents had when they were young and I had when I was a baby. All my pictures taken of me were taken from a box camera that you look down into! I don't think it's any different at all. There will be family albums, but this time they'll be video albums as opposed to still-picture albums.

SISKEL: When you see most people's home videos, do you want to say to them, "Why don't you just do this. It would make your film so much easier. Don't frame them in the center."

SPIELBERG: I try at almost all costs to avoid seeing peoples home videos, Gene, and I've been pretty good about avoiding it up to now! [Laughs]

SISKEL: That is the mistake, right? They frame everything dead center?

SPIELBERG: I don't know if there's any mistake so much. I think to people having a camcorder at home, it's just an extension of what they would choose to see. I have seen a couple of videos, and let's say they go to Disneyland. Well, they are so excited about being at Disneyland that there are a lot of whip pans. There's four seconds of this, and quickly two seconds of this, and then right down to the child crying, and then back up to Mickey Mouse, and back down to the child screaming, and back up to Mickey Mouse, back down to the child laughing, and back up to Mickey Mouse! The appetite to get it all in during the vacation creates a lot of panic. That's mainly what I see when I see videos like that!

SISKEL: And your advice would be, as you said to filmmakers . . .

SPIELBERG: No, no, no, at home my advice would be, "Do anything you want. Just shoot from the heart. Don't listen to us. Just make your own movies."

March 22, 1990

ROGER EBERT
INTERVIEWS
GEORGE LUCAS

ROGER EBERT: I want to start with what you said just before we sat
down, which is that for fifty years nobody was listening to the
audience, in terms of their appreciation of what was happening
technically in the theater.

GEORGE LUCAS: Well, I think the real issue is that the old adage that
the projectionist gets the final cut really goes beyond that, just
because it's really the theater owner and the manager and the
projectionist—it's their show. And we supply them with the
software. But at the same time it's only as good as the presentation that they give the audience. That involves the technology,
which is how much they spend on keeping their equipment up
and what kind of equipment they have, and just the sensitivity
toward the audience and what's happening with them. I think
it's vitally important to the enjoyment of movies. I've watched
lots of movies under lots of different conditions, and how a film
is presented has a great deal to do with your emotional response
to that movie and how much you enjoy it, how much you get
out of it.

EBERT: Describe for me a moviegoer's typical experience in movie
hell: the worst theater—in terms of things you've observed
involving projection, sound, and other things—that's out there
right now. What do they have to go through?

LUCAS: We have a few of them right around here! [Laughs] I don't even know where to start! The theater is incredibly dirty and smelly, and the air conditioning is very loud and sort of over-rides everything. And the room has not been acoustically treated, so the sound echoes through the room and sort of bounces around and it's hard to understand the dialogue. And then you start getting into the situations where people turn the lamp housings down or they don't have a sufficient lamp hous-ing, so that the image is very low. We've gone into theaters and checked them out where the light levels, the foot-candles, are at one-tenth what they should be. One-tenth!

EBERT: You mean the projectionist is turning down the light in the projector?

LUCAS: There is so little light that it's amazing there's any image on the screen at all.

EBERT: What if you're in a movie theater and you sense that it should be brighter. What should you do?

LUCAS: Well, I've been in situations where people have complained, and in some theaters the theater manager is responsive to that, and in other theaters they just don't care. And that's a tragedy because in developing the THX system and going around the country and then studying what people's reactions are to a really high-quality sound system and then trying to explain that to the theater owners to get more of them put in, we've discov-ered that twice as many people will go to a THX theater show-ing the same movie in the same city in the same quality theater. And it's just because they want it—they want the best possible presentation.

EBERT: People notice that.

LUCAS: People do notice it and they will pay for it. They will drive further. They will drive out of one area into another area to get a higher quality presentation. The same thing happened when I brought *Star Wars* out. Seventy-millimeter for all practical purposes was dead. Nobody was using it anymore. It was too expensive and it wasn't a big deal. So after a lot of pushing and shoving, I talked them into having, like, ten 70-millimeter prints, and doing it that way. So we had ten 70-millimeter prints; we had one here in San Francisco. And we found that people were flying in from Oregon and Washington and Arizona to see this print, because it was in eight-track stereo. It was really *the* presentation. People would fly from all over the country to see that.

EBERT: A lot of people know or would just assume that 70-millimeter is better than 35-millimeter, without knowing why. Could you tell us what the difference is?

LUCAS: Two main factors. One is that you have a bigger negative. You have a bigger image that's being projected through the lamp housing. It's a bigger transparency. It's the difference between having a 16-millimeter transparency, and projecting light through it, and one that's huge. You get a better rendition of everything. That's one factor. The other is the sound on "70" is magnetic sound, which means that you can get a higher quality than you can on optical sound. Optical is a photographic process; magnetic is what you have in your stereo system, with your magnetic tapes. And so you can get a better frequency range and that sort of thing.

EBERT: If we look forward to the next ten years, to the coming decade, as Doctor Lucas and his staff of skilled movie surgeons visit these wretched cinematic hells around the country and try to turn them into good theaters, what do you do? What do you prescribe for people when you go in and look at a theater?

LUCAS: Well, we have two programs at the company. One is the THX program, where we put together a speaker package, an acoustical package, and a general package for the theater. It's really a package of standards and some advanced technology, and it encompasses the whole area of presentation in a theater, not just a little computer chip or something that we've developed. And because we license it, we monitor it from time to time, to make sure that they keep the theater up to standard. And then after a period of time when their license is up, if they have slipped, then they lose their license. So it's a way of monitoring the theaters and helping them to maintain a standard. A lot of this is standard setting, just saying, "This is the standard." They have a *SMPTE* standard [the standard of the Society of Motion Picture and Television Engineers], but nobody paid much attention to it. And what we've done is modified it and made it more realistic and then presented it to the theater owners and helped them to bring their theater up to that standard. The THX system is basically a speaker system, but we always go in and redo the acoustics of the room—the walls and everything else—and check the air conditioning systems and all that, to make sure that it's up to standard.

EBERT: When we were downstairs being shown around, we were looking at the baffles made of wood blocks that were designed according to a mathematical formula to treat sound in a certain way. I imagine that a lot more is known about acoustics now than when most of these theaters were built.

LUCAS: Yeah, it's still a bit of a speculative science. And we're fortunate that we've had a great number of engineers, from Tom Holman, who developed the THX system, to George Massenberg, who developed the acoustic block system of recording. What we're able to do is take that expertise and knowledge and then bring it to architects and acoustical experts around the country who may not be aware of the state of the art and what's going on and how they can solve certain problems. In some cases when they're building theaters they don't bring in acoustical experts. Fortunately, if we're brought in as a theater chain is developing a new cineplex or a multiplex, we can be very helpful with the architects because we can help them cut costs and at the same time we can make the rooms acoustically more up to standard.

EBERT: One thing that I imagine directors didn't think a lot about fifty years ago, because they didn't have the tools to think

with, is what was demonstrated downstairs, the use of part of
the sound track to create an ambience that, in an aural sense,
includes the audience in the space that the character is in.
For example, you demonstrated the feeling that we're in that
underground cave with Indiana Jones in the clip that was rolled
downstairs. Is that something that has just come along recently?

LUCAS: No, surround sound has actually been here for a long time,
since the fifties, really. It came out with stereo. There was stereo
and then surround sound. And that's really surround sound. But
the aesthetics of doing that have evolved. The technology is not
the essence of the entertainment experience. It's what you do
with the technology, it's how you use that and how you manipulate it. It's not the paint and the canvas, it's the picture. The paint
and the canvas have been there a long time, but people didn't
really understand how to paint pictures with it. I've always
been very, very involved in sound and very interested in sound,
especially in relation to moving images, and so we have a rather
aggressive sound department here. We've put a lot of energy
into trying to understand the psychological effects and the
emotional effects of surround sound, and how it works on an
audience and what you can get away with and what you can't
get away with. We experiment with various movies. Sometimes
we'll do things that don't work, but we're always out there
trying to do things, to see what happens and then going into the
theater and seeing how people respond to those things. We're
very much into following up on an idea. We don't just do some
quickie idea on the sound track and then the movie goes out
and we forget about it. The movie goes out, we go out and see
what happened, see if it worked or it didn't work, see how
people responded to it. And if it works then we continue to use
that technique, and if it doesn't, we don't. We forget it.

EBERT: When I'm in a screening that I have any control over, such as
a press screening where I'm the only person there or it's a group
of us, I'm always saying things like, "It's too loud," or "It's not

loud enough," or "Are you sure this movie wasn't shot in stereo?" I can't tell you how many times over the years I've been sitting in a theater realizing I'm listening to a mono movie that was shot in stereo and the projectionist simply hasn't turned on the equipment correctly. And it frightens me to think how many people either don't really care about the quality of what's happening to them or don't know what's available.

LUCAS: I don't think people in general are sophisticated enough in the technology to realize when something's wrong. Even for a filmmaker it's hard sometimes to realize that something's not right, even when you're looking at your own film sometimes! You look at it and you say, "Wait a minute, the left channel's out here." Suddenly it throws you off. You don't quite know why you're being thrown off. It's a very delicate experience watching a movie, and most people don't realize that. It's not unless you get into having a film shown to you in a perfect, pristine condition, exactly the way it was meant to be, and then seeing it in another condition where everything is screwy, that you begin to realize that the whole experience drops dramatically, that the enjoyment of the movie and the understanding of the movie and the impact and the emotional sway of the film is completely altered depending on how many speakers are working and how dim the image is and whether you can pick up the little nuances of what is on the film. For example, that his hand went over and touched her knee at that particular point. If you don't know that, if you didn't see it because it got too dark then, or you missed a key piece of dialogue, such as who murdered who, suddenly the movie's a different experience.

EBERT: In your films, you've spent a lot of time filling the frame and filling the space around the characters with details that are fun to find and fun to observe and fun to see: little creatures, a little something going on in the background or a little action going on over here. That is lost frequently not only because of bad projection but also because when people look at them at home the

picture's been cropped so that maybe the center of action is
there, but the context is floating somewhere in space on either
side of the television set. That must really be frustrating for you.

LUCAS: It is, it is. It's very frustrating, and that's why I've put as
much time into how the audience sees the film as I have. Because it's not enough to actually create an interesting experience, it's very important for you to hope that the audience is
getting that same experience. And up to a few years ago it's been
a very difficult thing to do, and nobody's been monitoring it.
Stanley Kubrick would come out and he'd try to check some
theaters, but it's been a very ad hoc thing done primarily by
the filmmakers, because they're the ones that have the most
concern about it. And they're the ones that understand the relationship between the technology and the psychology of the
audience. So they're the ones that are pushing it the most. The
studios just look at it as a sort of bottom-line expense, and they
don't understand that relationship quite as well.

EBERT: If you could forget about evolutionary progress altogether
and just leap ahead with a dream list of things to do, what
would be the ideal experience you could give an audience in a
movie theater, in terms of projection and sound and how they're
seated and how they're presented with it? If you could just start
from scratch; you wouldn't have to work with existing projectors, you wouldn't have to work with anything that exists now,
and you could assume everything you needed had been
invented.

LUCAS: That's a hard question. [Laughs] It's hard to leap that far
forward because it's hard to know exactly what is going to
happen. Having things standardized is one of the more important issues. We've got screening rooms here that are really as
near perfect a screening room as you can get. And when we
show a movie in there it's an amazing experience. Then you can
go down the street to a regular movie theater and it's not the
same experience. I'm just hoping that for the mass theaters, we

could get them up to the level that you can get them up to now. If you just take the time and the money and the effort to do, it would be a great leap forward in the moviegoing experience for people.

EBERT: When people begin to have high definition television in their homes so that they can look at a television picture or a home video or a video-movie on a screen that is ten feet wide, and they have surround sound, maybe even your THX surround sound system, what, if anything, are you going to do to encourage them to feel that they still have to go out of their home to see your movies in first run?

LUCAS: Well, I think the marketplace will shift dramatically in that situation. I think certain kinds of movies will be made directly for the home and certain kinds of movies will be made for theater presentation. No matter how you get around it the theater presentation is a group experience, and there is something very magical about a group experience. You cannot duplicate it in the home unless you invite five hundred of your closest friends in! But short of that people are going to continue, I think, to go to the group experience. It's the difference between watching a football game on television and going to a football game. There is a definite difference in the energy level and just all the stuff that goes on. You enjoy both of them in different ways. But people don't stop actually going to experience the event first-hand. I think that will continue with the movies.

EBERT: Do you think in the age of high definition television that theatrical movies will tend to be more spectacular?

LUCAS: Yeah, the larger, more spectacular ones will end up in the theater and the more personal ones will end up on the screen. Which is good, because it will allow more esoteric movies into the marketplace. We're in a period now where the industry is such that they are going toward a higher end kind of movie, and the high-risk movies are not getting a lot of play now. And that's real unfortunate.

EBERT: The strange thing is, when you were making *Star Wars* it was a high-risk movie.

LUCAS: Oh yeah, it was very high risk. Science fiction had never done that well, except for maybe *Planet of the Apes*. And *2001* had a very shaky history. And there really wasn't anything else. The highest grossing science fiction film was $60 million or something like that, in rentals. It was very high risk to do what was then a $10 million space adventure. Nobody understood the script. Nobody understood what it was, what the market was for it. They perceived it as a young person's movie. Not necessarily a children's film, but basically for younger people. And that made them extremely nervous. It's amazing that it *was* basically a young person's movie and it was extremely successful. Then Steve [Steven Spielberg] went along and tried to do *E.T.*, and Columbia didn't make it for the same reason. "This is a young person's movie, and we know what the top end for one of that kind of movie is," which is *Star Wars,* but they always think of it as "Disney." There are two ways of looking at those situations.

EBERT: You believe that the current videotape-rental system will become obsolete. What's it going to be replaced by?

LUCAS: Pay-per-view. I mean, why would you go down to a video store when you can get the same movie piped into your home for two bucks? And you could charge it.

EBERT: And you choose the movie you want, right?

LUCAS: You choose the movie you want. And they come on probably at set times, but also I think there will be a system where you just get charged for a movie. What I think will probably happen is that the capacity of cable's going into the home is go-- ing to expand vastly when fiber optics come in. And you will be able at that point to just dial up the movie that you want. It will be shown at particular times, but I think you'll be able to dial it up in two ways. You'll be able to pay two dollars or something for it and see it, but you won't be able to copy it. It will be uncopyable. Or you'll be able to pay, you know, twenty dollars for it, and you can copy it. Which means you can do it just like you do any television show: You just plug it in, put your tape in, set the timer, dial it up, and when you come home you've got the cassette there. You don't have to go out and buy it in a store.

EBERT: The other night I was in L.A. and I rented and looked at *The Fountainhead.* I think I must have been the only person in Los Angeles on that evening who wanted to see *The Fountainhead.* If I had this fiber optic system, would it be able to cater to my desire to see such a movie? Or would it only be a hits-driven system?

LUCAS: No, I think eventually it can be a system that you can get anything on. You'll be able to call up any particular subject matter, and anywhere. You'll be able to roam through it. There'll be services offered to you, you know, various companies. Basically what you'll do is you'll plug into companies that have those films in their libraries. And those libraries will be on disc. In all probability when you record them at home you'll be recording them on disc, and not on tape. It's kind of what they're trying to do a little bit in record stores now. There's certain technology where you can go and make your own tapes, and it's also there to make your own discs.

EBERT: And it'll be a high definition disc.

LUCAS: Yeah, probably all high definition.

EBERT: So an ordinary person in an ordinary place could have a home-movie library that would be the envy of a major studio mogul from 1945.

LUCAS: Yeah, you'll probably have a computer catalog on your television, and you'll be able to go through it alphabetically, or arranged to Westerns or foreign films or anything you want, any kind of subject matter: films about tennis, films about this . . . Punch it up, see a long list of films, punch up the film, find out more information about it—the biography of it—and then, if you really like it, punch it up and get a preview of it. And if you like that, then you could order it.

EBERT: Most of the filmmakers I've spoken to, though, really feel that at this point at least, they still want to stick with film because video just doesn't look good enough projected or shown on a big screen. The *Julia and Julia* experiment, for example, didn't convince too many people.

LUCAS: Right. The technology is not there yet. But what we're talking about is like early color, with people looking at it and saying, "It's never going to replace black and white. Forget it. It's too garish, it's too hard to control. You can't tell a story that way." In that particular case aesthetically it completely upset the language of film, because the language was a black and white language and the graphic art of gray and darks and lights and everything was based on black and white. And when you introduce color into it, it destroys that, and so the very essence of it was being challenged. As well as the fact that the technology wasn't there and early color films look completely goofy. And that's where we are right now with video. But you have to look ten, twenty years ahead. I know for a fact that they will have video to the quality of the best film that we have today. It may not get up there with Showscan or some of the really high-tech stuff, but the normal 35-millimeter image will definitely be available on video before the twenty-first century. [Showscan is a system in which a 70-millimeter film print is projected at sixty frames per second rather than at the current theatrical standard of twenty-four frames per second.]

EBERT: Somebody was telling me that the problem of video right now is that it drops off to black and white at either end without going through as much gray as film does.

LUCAS: Yeah, but again the potential electronically is enormous. We're just on the very leading edge of a whole technology. Whereas running celluloid through gears is really in the end a nineteenth-century technology. I think they've pretty much pushed that to the limit. I don't see that going much further.

EBERT: Will this take us finally to the vision that Francis Coppola was drawing for me in 1967 when he opened up his briefcase and pulled out all of these catalogues and said, "The day's going to come when every man can walk around with a motion picture studio on his shoulder?"

LUCAS: We have that today. It's the highest rated television show in America.

EBERT: [Laughs] "America's Funniest Home Videos."

LUCAS: That's it.

EBERT: A little quality control is needed, though.

LUCAS: Quality control is a little shaky! There's a short form right now, but hey, they can move that to half an hour. They can move it to an hour, then they can move it to two hours. And what you shoot with your little 8-millimeter camera is one level of quality, but that's going to evolve. People will have high definition home video cameras that are like Video 8's. What the issue really gets down to in all of this is it's like writing. Anybody can write. Very few people can write well. It's going to be the same thing with film. Once you develop literacy for all the people and give them the technology—the pencils or whatever—then it's just a matter of who can do it well and who can't. Most people can't.

EBERT: That's a good point. The invention of the typewriter didn't lead to a flood of great novels.

LUCAS: That's right.

EBERT: Same number of great novels as before the typewriter.

LUCAS: Because it's not the machinery, it's the mind behind the machinery that makes it count. It's an art and a talent. It's not something you can just come to.

EBERT: Now what about interactive video? I know that you once, probably in a moment of self-indulgent fantasy, said that you were almost tempted to just go into interactive video and stop making movies.

LUCAS: Actually, I've done that for the last year. I've been working

on interactive video. It's really for learning systems for the
schools.

EBERT: Let's start by a definition of what interactive video means to
you.

LUCAS: The type of interactive video that I'm working on is a com-
bination of the computer and a video disc, so that you have a
library of visual information that you can manipulate using a
computer. The process of combining video disc technology
with computer technology opens up a whole avenue—in the
area I'm working in, in terms of education—of ways of teaching
and having kids be involved in a curiosity-based learning experience, rather than somebody just giving you information in a
normal documentary film or a lecture.

EBERT: So what does a kid do when he uses the system that you've
been working on?

LUCAS: We're developing various levels of systems that are interactive; they're all interactive. I have two groups. One is a games
group, which develops video games, and the other is the learning group, which develops computer and interactive technology
for the schools. I've been developing the school technology for
about five years, but I have taken the last year off to devote a
huge amount of my time to it. The prototype that we have that's
the farthest out and actually working at this point, is a half-hour
science lecture for high school science. It combines a lecture
with a dramatization with documentary footage, and you can
access all this footage in a structured way. In this particular case
the subject is heredity and DNA, and the discovery of DNA. So
that you get into this lecture and study DNA and then you go
and you see a dramatization of these people trying to discover it.
In the process of trying to discover it you begin to understand
what it is, because you have to go through the process of what
they're trying to discover. Then there is a work station where
you can see a double helix and where the genes are on the coil
and all that. You can pull it apart like in the computer and that

sort of thing. In some of the other systems we're developing
there are games. That system we developed with the Smithso-
nian. We're developing another system with the Audubon
Society right now, a system about a swamp or a lake, where all
the ducks on the lake disappear. You're supposed to try to figure out what happened to the ducks! You get to interview the
farmer that lives next door and the wildlife forest ranger—this is
his area—and the people that run the munitions plant down the
road. You get to go around and find out what caused all the
ducks to disappear.

EBERT: Now could it have been the farmer, the forest ranger, or the
munitions plant? [Laughs]

LUCAS: But you get an interview with each person. You get to
actually talk to them and ask them questions and they answer
you. So you try to see if you can figure out what it is. It's a very
exciting kind of system. It's a very elaborate outgrowth of gam-
ing, or it's an interactive movie in which you can actually talk
to the characters and ask them questions and get answers and
based on that make various decisions and move along.

EBERT: We were downstairs looking at an editor demonstrate the
laser disc editing system in which he can go from one cut to
another cut instantly, even though they're not adjacent on the
disc, because the disc has instant access. Presumably you could
go one more step, couldn't you? And have an interactive movie
where we could be deciding along with Luke Skywalker what
was going to happen next. Or we could make a turn to the right
or a turn to the left or decide to fire or decide not to fire or do
things like this. Is that plausible?

LUCAS: It's plausible. The aesthetics of that are as yet to be deter-
mined, I think.

EBERT: Yet the whole idea of a movie experience is that the director
tells you what's going to happen next.

LUCAS: Yeah. Movies are basically storytelling. You're telling a story
and you're guiding the people through a particular kind of expe-

rience. So how that operates with interactive is an area that's never been explored. We don't know how to do that, and it will be very interesting to see. What I'm doing in terms of interactive education is very much in that mode, but it's directed at teaching, not at giving you a particular emotional experience. The ability to develop an emotional experience in audiences is very tightly controlled—unbelievably controlled, that is to say, even to the point of the amount of light level that ends up on the screen, and whether you can hear all the words clearly. I mean, if you've been through a sound mix, just how high the footsteps are helps to create that particular emotional experience that you're going through. Obviously it's the history of movies and the history of editing and the history of photography and art in general: How do you evoke a particular emotion in the viewer using color, light, and sound, and that sort of thing? And in this case, pacing and rhythm. The exciting thing about film is it combines all the arts. It has all of the basic rules that music has combined with all the basic rules of graphic arts and the literary arts. You really have a large playing field. But when you put the elements together you have to be extremely controlled. It's like playing a piece of music. You can't have interactive music. You can, but it's a different aesthetic experience from listening to a symphony.

EBERT: You can't tell a story to yourself, or at least not in the same way that somebody can tell it to you.

LUCAS: No, you can't. I mean, you can. That is to say, you can sit down at the piano and play your own tune, if you want.

EBERT: And doodle around.

LUCAS: It's different from listening to a symphony play something that somebody has created.

EBERT: Looking at a scene from *Indiana Jones,* which you wrote, I think it would be very frustrating for you, the filmmaker, if I, the viewer, had some buttons and I said, "I don't think I want him to jump over that chasm. I think I want him to let the stone wall fall down, and he'll turn around and look around and see what's happening on this side." You would say, "No, because if you do that you're not going to get the scene where the big ball rolls down."

LUCAS: No, no, as a storyteller it's definitely frustrating. But it's more frustrating for the audience than it would be for the person who's trying to tell the story. It's just as if I were to sit down and tell you a story, and you interrupted me every five minutes and said, "Well, no, I don't want that. I want him to do this." I'd say, "Wait a minute, I'm telling the story!"

EBERT: [Laughs]

LUCAS: We have *Indiana Jones* video games. They're just like that. You can get the *Last Crusade* video game and go through the movie and it's basically a similar plot. But at any given point you can go off and do something else. You can fail to make connections that Indiana Jones makes or decide not to make those connections and you end up in a completely different adventure. In a video game that's perfectly acceptable, because you're not telling a story, you're playing a game. It's a different psychological experience. And it works pretty well. For people who have seen the movie it's fun because then they get to explore other aspects that they weren't aware of in the movie. And it's a fun game that way, but as a primary experience in terms of storytelling it just won't work. That isn't the way storytelling is. But it will be a valid form of art or entertainment at some point in the future. It is now, and that form is basically video games. What we're doing is, instead of having relatively crude visualizations of things on the screen, we're able to take that and use the video disc and give you movie-quality visualizations.

EBERT: Even on the computer screen.

LUCAS: Yeah, on a computer screen. No, that's the difference of it.

EBERT: It's been about seven years since the last *Star Wars* movie. It was '83, was it?

LUCAS: Yeah, '83.

EBERT: I understand that you're finally going to go back into that universe.

LUCAS: Yeah, obviously I have these stories, and I've been trying to figure out a time when I'm going to devote a serious amount of time to bringing these next three stories to the screen. It's a big challenge, and I've had a lot of other things that I've been interested in other than to devote my life to that. I've started to work on trying to evolve how I'm going to do the next three and what I'm going to do with them. It hopefully will happen sometime in the next five to seven years.

EBERT: When you started on the *Star Wars* saga, you had nine stories altogether in your mind.

LUCAS: No, what really happened was I wrote a screenplay. The screenplay was way too big. And so what I decided to do was take the first act of that screenplay and make it into a movie. That's what I did with *Star Wars*. But in order to create that script, I had done a lot of back stories to get me to that place. Because it's sort of like you come in at the middle of the movie. So I developed all of those back stories to understand where the characters went and how they did what they did and all that stuff. I had to figure out everything that went before it. *Star Wars* was the first act of that screenplay and then *Empire* and *Jedi* went on and completed that screenplay. Then at the end I found that I also had this whole other story that had been created. There was basically enough for three more movies from the back story that I had created in order to create the first one. That's really where that came from. Then at some point somebody said, "Well, couldn't you continue on?" And I thought it would be interesting someday to do one that had all of my characters from the first film in their sixties and seventies, and dealing with what went on at that time, because it's a generational movie.

EBERT: But *Star Wars, Empire,* and *Jedi* are really four, five, and six. And you're now thinking of doing one, two, and three.

LUCAS: Yeah, because I have all the information on that and I know the stories.

EBERT: Do they take place earlier in the life span of the characters in four, five, and six?

LUCAS: Yeah. It's really about Obi-Wan Kenobi as a boy.

EBERT: I can't imagine him as a boy!

LUCAS: Yeah, well, he was a boy and so was Anakin Skywalker, who became Darth Vader eventually. It's those characters and how they ended up getting where they were. The number three film is the one that Luke gets born in, so there's about a twenty-year stretch between three and four [*Star Wars,* in which Luke Skywalker is about twenty years old]. I would say that those three [*Star Wars, The Empire Strikes Back,* and *Return of the Jedi*] happen in about ten years or something. Maybe not quite that long.

EBERT: In the original *Star Wars* trilogy, the success of the first one gave you the money for the second two, to really do almost anything. I know for the first film, Fox was kind of giving you five dollars at a time at the end. You created films that were probably as difficult and exhausting to make as any films ever made, in terms of the painstaking work involved. And after you finished the third one you were at least quoted as saying that you had had it for a while. That you were tired.

LUCAS: I *was* tired. [Laughs] I'd really been through the wringer doing those three movies. It's a very difficult, life-consuming experience. And by that time I had a family and everything and I was really interested in not dropping off the face of the earth just to do three more of them. I'd kind of done it, and I'd had the experience and there were a lot of other things I wanted to do in life. Until I could figure out a way of managing to do another series, I was just going to go along doing what I was doing at that point, which was producing.

EBERT: You've really created this entire Skywalker Ranch since then, in terms of it being a functioning entity. Is this in one sense a

tool to allow you to make the next three movies with less personal drain?

LUCAS: Well, it's partially a tool. I'm not sure how it's going to work
out, because the main part of the tool is the production facility
which I'm trying to build down the road, which has been
stalled for the last two or three years. Whether or not I'm ever
going to get to do it is sort of dubious at this point. And that
relates to being able to do the next *Star Wars*. They're all connected, so I'm trying to resolve developing a facility that will
allow me to make the next one and then trying to deal with the
real problem, which is writing it and telling the story and that
sort of thing. At the same time, I'm getting to the point now
where I'm starting to evolve the story and hoping this other
thing resolves itself at some point.

EBERT: Are you kind of daunted? I mean, it's almost like the runner
getting back into shape again after winning the marathon and
sitting around for seven years. This is obviously going to be an
enormous slice of the nineties for you personally, this project
[of shooting the first movies in the *Star Wars* saga].

LUCAS: What I've been trying to work on is to be able to do it so it's
not a big slice of the nineties for me, to be able to do it so that
I can deal with it financially, because the costs of doing these
kinds of movies has just gone completely through the roof. If
I were to try to do a *Return of the Jedi* today using the same
technology and the same techniques that I used seven years
ago—and those films are made as efficiently as you can possibly
make a movie; I had a well-honed crew that had worked over
nine years together and they were really sharp and everything
was done in a highly efficient manner with no money wasted—
to do that movie today would cost, I would say, at least $75
million.

EBERT: You're kidding!

LUCAS: No.

EBERT: But yet in seven years there's been so much advance in the computer technology. When you made *Star Wars,* the first picture, the personal computer didn't exist, for example.

LUCAS: But the thing of it is that computer technology isn't really to a point now where it's cost effective. We do a lot of computer graphics at ILM [Industrial Light & Magic, Lucasfilm Ltd.'s special-effects division] and we're really one of the leaders, but the truth of it is the cost to do that is still greater than if you were to do it just in the old-fashioned way.

EBERT: With models and back projection.

LUCAS: You can see that the future will be there. And as I say, the cost will come down, the storage capacity will get greater, the technology will advance and then it will be the medium that takes over. There's no doubt about that. But right now—well, let's just say, five years ago it was just astronomically different. It would cost three or four times as much to do it with a computer as it did to do it just the old-fashioned way. Now it's beginning to run pretty much neck and neck. It's still more expensive in the computer, but it's getting to the point where it's getting very close. I would say within five years the computer technology will be cheaper than the old-fashioned way.

EBERT: This is amusing because people are so willing to casually say, "Oh, it's all done on computers." Whatever you're talking about, people say, "Oh, it's all done on computers these days." And it isn't all done on computers yet!

LUCAS: Believe me, I've been involved in a lot of state-of-the-art computer technology, and you'd be surprised what they can't do. [Laughs] They've got a ways to go. They *will* be able to do it, but they can't do it right now.

EBERT: Your first *Star Wars* picture of the next trilogy will obviously not be budgeted at $75 million.

LUCAS: No, no. And the thing is, those costs are not special effects, although that's a big hunk of it. Special effects on a movie like, say, *Return of the Jedi* are, I would say, about 20 percent of the budget. That's a pretty good chunk, considering. But it's still only 20 percent, and you have 80 percent of the other things, which is the cast and the crew and the transportation costs and building the sets, and just all the other things that you've got that go into a movie. Those are the things that are really expensive. That's where the cost has risen. When I did the first *Star Wars,* it was $10 million. It was the same thing with *Raiders.* When we did *Raiders* it was $20 million. And they were pretty much the same scale, pretty much done the same way. *Raiders* was especially telling because we did all three of them pretty much in the same way for the same amount of money. But the truth of it is that just inflation would add on about $10 million a year. Ten million dollars a year!

EBERT: Your first two features, *THX-1138* and *American Graffiti,* were what could be called "personal" films.

LUCAS: Well, *THX* especially was a personal film in that that was the kind of movie making I liked to do and was doing at the time. I really saw myself when I got out of school as being a cinema verité documentary filmmaker, who on the side was able to make these sort of personal movies, visual films, which a lot of my friends up here in San Francisco were doing, and the Canadian Film Board was doing, and something I was just emotionally connected with. And I loved cinema verité. Then I got an opportunity to do a theatrical feature, which was about the last thing from my mind, really. But since the opportunity presented itself I took it, just to see what I could do. That was taking my personal kind of vision and trying to translate it to the theatrical medium, and with dubious success, but it was an interesting experiment. *American Graffiti* on the other hand was after I'd finished that [*THX-1138*] under Francis [Coppola] who then said, "Look, why don't you try to do just a real movie? You know, a real theatrical movie in the tradition of theatrical movies. Forget all this other stuff that you're doing. Just try to do a regular movie where there are a lot of human beings and actors and they act, and it's funny, and it's like a real

movie." So that was the challenge there. I obviously took something out of my past and I made something that I cared about.
But in a way part of it was a challenge to learn theatrical filmmaking. I did that, and found myself when I finished it not
being very well regarded by the studio, and whether it was
going to be released was dubious. I hadn't made any money
and so I was dead broke and I needed to get a new job. So that's
when I got the job to do this space fantasy that I wanted to do,
which was based on the idea of doing a kind of modern fairy
tale adventure movie, the kind that I grew up on, which was
basically Westerns. I got this job because I needed the job,
basically. That's what got me into *Star Wars* in the first place.
And I really intended at some point to turn around and get back
and do what I wanted to do.

EBERT: I was going to say, *American Graffiti* is a film that is a
starting point for a career that you haven't had yet.

LUCAS: Pretty much.

EBERT: A different career. As a different filmmaker.

LUCAS: Yeah. My career has sort of gone sideways. I don't know
why, other than that I did what seemed to be right at the
moment and what seemed to be the thing I needed to do. I
never really thought about where my career was going or what
my reputation would be or what I'd be thought of afterward.
The truth is, right after *THX* I developed *Apocalypse Now* and I
couldn't get it off the ground. So then I did *American Graffiti*.
Then I tried to get *Apocalypse Now* off the ground again.
Couldn't do it. So then I did *Star Wars*. And about halfway
through *Star Wars* Francis came to me and said, "Look, I'll
finance this [*Apocalypse Now*] myself now. No studio will ever
finance this film. I've got the money. I've finished *The God-
father;* I'll do it." And *American Graffiti* was a success and it
looked like maybe there was a way of putting [my own production of *Apocalypse Now*] together, but I'd already spent a year
of my life working on *Star Wars,* and I decided I was going to

continue with that. A lot of my friends at the time after *Star Wars* were saying, "Why don't you do a movie like *Taxi Driver?* Why don't you do some artistic statement? Why are you making children's films? This is completely lunatic." And I said, "Well, I want to do it. I'd like to do *Apocalypse,* because it's a film I really care about, and I'd like to make it. But I'm already into this [*Star Wars*]. Even though I had a screenplay finished on *Apocalypse,* I had a crew [for *Star Wars*] and I was on my way! So I said, "I just can't drop this at this point. I'll do it after *Star Wars,* but I won't do it before." So it was that sort of bad timing thing that sent me off in that direction instead of this direction. Then once I'd done *Star Wars* the possibility of actually continuing the series and being able to get the whole original idea done was too overwhelming. Then I really decided, "This is what I'm going to do." That's how I moved from being a director to a producer, because I realized I wasn't going to be able to finish the other two as a director. I really needed to be more overseeing of things, and more all-encompassing than just being the director, where I have a tendency to be very focused on what happens in a very specific area on the set.

EBERT: In your desk over there in the bottom drawer do you have any scripts that have been there for a while? That might not take $50 million to make?

LUCAS: There is a script that's been sitting around since the *American Graffiti* days. In order to do *American Graffiti* I had to sell my life to Universal, and as a consequence of that I developed a screenplay that I was very interested in at the time that I was going to direct. It's called *Radioland Murders,* which is a murder mystery comedy, just a complete wacko comedy. It's been sitting there for fifteen years. It may get done, actually. I pull it out every once in a while and see if I can get somebody to direct it. Nobody's that interested, or nobody's connected with it yet. That's the same thing that happened in *Raiders.* That was something I had sitting on the shelf, and nobody wanted to do it and somebody would come in and say, "Well, maybe," and spend a week or two on it. Then finally when I poked it in front of Steve's face he went berserk and said, "Let's do it! Let's do it!" Otherwise it'd still be sitting on the shelf along with *Radioland Murders*!

EBERT: Is there a moment in your work that crystalizes George Lucas the filmmaker?

LUCAS: I don't know. That's very difficult, because I don't know whether it's an image in any of the films. I'm trying to think back. That's a hard one to pull off the top of your head. There are moments that I love in the movies. I'm a very strong believer in knowing a lot of filmmakers personally, and I see their personalities in their movies and they *are* definitely reflected in their movies in a very strong way. But what is reflected is a part of their psychology that you can't really talk about unless you actually know that particular person. You could take all of somebody's work and then begin to find the psychological thread that runs through it. There definitely is one, and it reflects their personalities completely. But it's the whole thing. It's really the whole body of their work rather than just seeing one image. I think for me it's a pace and an editorial style more than it is an actual photographic image that is the essence of what I am. [Laughs]

EBERT: I was trying in my own mind to think. One of my favorite moments in your work of course, is when the cops take off in *American Graffiti* and they lose their back axle. Which psychologically might be telling us, "Not so fast. Make sure that you have the technological system all figured out before you step on the accelerator." But then, of course that's stretching it.

LUCAS: Yeah, I could find lots of images. Again, when you boil it down I have lots of themes that run through all my movies, the same theme and lots of things that I care about that I include.

EBERT: But it's more the pacing, you think.

LUCAS: But if you're saying that "Here is a frame and this is an image," in thinking of just a graphic depiction of something it's hard for me to come up with one that I would say, "That sums up the way I feel about things." But I've noticed that the one thing that I bring to the medium that is unique to me is that sort of pace and editorial style, which probably reflects my personality.

EBERT: Can you give us a series of four shots that embody your pace and editorial style?

LUCAS: A series of shots?

EBERT: Yeah. We'd have to have more than one shot if we're going to talk about pacing.

LUCAS: Yes. Well, the only thing that comes to mind is a very odd little sequence in *Star Wars,* where they escape from the Death Star and they're shooting the TIE Fighters—they're in the Millennium Falcon—and they're in their gun ports. That little gun port sequence is, I think, an example of that.

EBERT: One other thing. What about the film-school notion that the area just to the right of center is an important area in a rectangular composition, and that you either move off of that in order to create tension or you put somebody there when they're at rest? This painting on the wall, for example, has its main vertical axis on the point just to the right of center. Do you ever think about it?

LUCAS: Well, that's not a film-school idea, that's an art-school idea. And the same rules that apply to fine art apply to film in the photographic arts. Obviously all these rules are being pushed every day. That's what the artist does is to push the rules. And obviously in graphics what's aesthetically pleasing is to not be on dead center, to be off. Again the interesting thing about film is that it's a more active medium, and it's a more international active medium, which means you get a much more direct response on a more subconscious level from an audience in terms of things like graphics and style. It's interesting, because the way we Westerners look at graphics is different from the way Easterners look at graphics. It's very interesting to see that some of the rules that are applied to Western art don't apply in other parts of the world. And that particular case is probably one of them. I'm a big fan of wide screen. I've shot all my films in wide screen, and many of my friends don't like that. They hate wide screen. They can't deal with it. But one of the essences of wide screen is playing with that particular rule. My first film, *THX,* is the most extreme in that way. I really played with the concept of where you are in the frame. And I put everything way off to the final tenth of the screen, or put something dead center. There are no rules when it really gets down to it. It's just what can you get away with.

EBERT: There are rules, but you don't have to follow them. And by not following them you can make them work for you even more than if you do follow them.

LUCAS: You can make something that's as aesthetically pleasing as if you did follow them. You have to be aware of them, though. You can do things by accident, but film is too complicated, if you're really going to have a fine film. People try to talk—when we were down there at the Academy—about Kurasawa and what makes him a great director. The only way I could explain it in a traditional media sound bite was to say that he was really a director's director. If you really understood directing and film-making, you then began to appreciate what he's able to bring to the game, because he can bring it better than anybody. There are other directors who have managed that level; I think Orson Welles did. But there are very few people who have command of the medium the way he does in all aspects. It's not just the graphics, but the graphics are cinematic graphics, which means graphics in motion. He really understands it, and that's the other issue: the other thing about being a third in the frame. Everything has to do with editing, because what you're doing is juxtaposing two images on top of each other, and it's where your eye goes. We had a couple of classes in it in school, and one

of them was Graphics in Motion, that Les Novros taught. It was
really a great course.

EBERT: Movement to movement, and how you can do that.

LUCAS: Movement to movement, and then the graphic design of
things coming toward you and things going away from you, and
just how you translate still graphic dynamics into a progressive
form. And what that does is when you replace one image with
another image very fast, which is an editorial cinematic technique. There's a lot of theory in all that, and some of it's very
true. And there are a lot of very involved psychological things
that happen just watching people's eyes move. We did an exer-
cise where you photograph people watching the image and
watching cuts, and watching what happens to their eyes when
you cut from somebody over here to somebody over there.
That all has an effect emotionally. There are a lot of ways you
can have people look directly into the camera, or slightly off;
how far off center you have them elicits a definite emotional
response in the audience in how much you relate to that particular character. Those are things that can be used. And those are
things that I think really, when you get into the more sophisticated end of filmmaking, film school does help you with. You'd
be surprised at the little subtle emotional things you can do: to
have one character always look right at the camera and the other
character looking off the camera and what that does to create
that character, because you really get a sense of a certain kind of
character that way. Or you have one character always looking
sort of off until the climactic scene, and then suddenly he's
looking at the camera and it heightens the impact.

EBERT: The audience has processed that in terms of what they think
about the character without ever having thought about it.

LUCAS: Yeah.

EBERT: "He's not looking at me."

LUCAS: Everything matters! And nothing matters.

EBERT: They say that people walking toward each other on a sidewalk can determine whether the other person is looking at them sooner than they can determine if they even recognize the other person!

LUCAS: Yeah.

EBERT: We are so incredibly cued into eyes. I don't know if it's George Lucas or not but I can already see if you're looking at me or not.

LUCAS: Well, it's also the same thing. Or you can tell by posture, sometimes.

EBERT: Let's move a little bit into preservation for a second here, first on a personal basis and then on the basis of what you directors as a group are trying to do with the studios. What as far as you know is being done to preserve your films so that they are available more or less in the form in which you directed them for fifty or one hundred years from now?

LUCAS: In the current system there's very little that assures that the people are going to see your work the way you intended it to be. I have quite a bit of control over taking care of my negatives and preserving the films. I have three-strip process on all my films. I'm assuming that at some point computer technology will come along and be able to tape this analog information and put it into a really sophisticated digital mode, so I try to get the best analog reproduction of what I've got.

EBERT: Three-strip means that the color won't fade because you can always take the three strips in order to make the color new again.

LUCAS: It's a printing process. It's like printing a magazine, basically. You have three different color strips. It's exactly like printing a magazine. You just run three colors and eventually it prints it into a final thing. Most films aren't done that way anymore. It's a process that was used with Technicolor for a number of years. It was very effective. And then they stopped it, but I have continued it through all my movies. In the last few years it's been impossible because now the system has been shipped to China and that's the only place it exists. But there's new technology that sort of compensates for that in some of the new negative that's being produced. I've always done everything I could to preserve my films in any way I can. But I have a limited number of films, and I have the wherewithal to do it. The big concern, I think, is with all the rest of the movies and what happens to them. And it's our heritage. It's a very valuable thing, and it's a shame to see it just drift away. I think most people are shocked when they realize that movies disappear. That they just disappear! Somebody's heard about a movie, they go to look, and they discover it doesn't exist anymore. It's gone.

EBERT: Most people are shocked to find out the movies even exist, because they think that they're just there in the theater somehow.

LUCAS: Yeah.

EBERT: They don't think that a can is carried from the airplane by somebody.

LUCAS: Yeah.

EBERT: When we first talked in Washington with you three guys, Spielberg at that point was saying that Universal had just discovered that the original negative of *Jaws* was in terrible shape. Now, Universal has been under the same management ever since it made *Jaws*. *Jaws* was one of the most successful movies ever made. They would have every interest in preserving it. And yet it was in a state of disrepair. What kind of thinking goes into this? Do they only think about new production? Don't they think about the investment of capital in preservation of their assets, of their past?

LUCAS: Well, the position in the film business is, once you show the movie in the theater, then that's it, it's dead. And then in the fifties they began to realize that, well, maybe it's not dead. Maybe if you put it on television it might have another life. And then they said, "Fine, that's right. But then you've sold the television rights and then it's dead and we don't worry about it

anymore." Then all of a sudden they invented videocassettes
and they said, "Oh, well, it's not really dead now!" And slowly
it's dawning on people that actually these films have a life. They
can go on for hundreds, if not thousands of years! But nobody's
paid any attention to it because it hasn't been of any value to
anybody. And now ultimately those film libraries are the only
things that are getting sold. When they sell a studio they don't
sell anything but the library. That's the only thing that has any
value. Yet they don't spend any money trying to preserve their
films. It's insane, but it's very consistent with the American
society. We value the least those things which are the most
meaningful to us, or the most valuable to us in a real sense:
teachers, nurses, mothers, films. Studios say, "We can't spend
a million dollars a year to have a staff take care of it, because
that's overhead. We've got to keep the overhead down."

EBERT: That's funny, too, when you consider the general studio
attitude toward overhead, which is very loose. As indicated in
the audit of the *Coming to America* saga, a lot of things were
charged to overhead; it's just too bad they didn't go ahead and
charge the vaults to overhead while they were charging everything else to overhead.

LUCAS: Well, they charge pretty much everything they can get away
with. It's hard to charge a vault to overhead and put it on the
movie.

EBERT: Yeah, I guess that's right.

LUCAS: It may seem that the studios are very loose, but when you
actually get down to the numbers and everything, what they're
charging are legitimate things that they can get away with charging. It seems unreasonable if you're on the other end of it and
being taken advantage of.

EBERT: You have a group of directors who have gone to the studios
to encourage them to preserve this heritage. Could you tell me
who you're working with and what you're doing and what
you're telling the studios?

LUCAS: The truth of it is that's more Marty's [Martin Scorsese's] thing than it is mine. I'm helping him with it, but Marty's trying to develop an archive and trying to get the studios to go back into their negatives and to make new negatives and new prints. It's a way of trying to force the studios to put some money back into their archives and pay more attention to them. That's the thrust that Marty has been going on and that I feel very strongly about and have been supportive of him, and helping him. The other end of it, which is the end that I've been more involved in—and Steve's been supportive of both of these things—is the artist's rights: the right of the filmmaker to have his film be preserved as he originally intended it and not have people be able to make changes to it and then still ascribe it as his work. That's a whole other legislative battle that's been going on over the last five years. It's one thing to get the studios to preserve the films, it's another thing to get them to legally *have* to preserve them exactly the way the filmmaker intended them, and not change them.

EBERT: The film in many cases will be the property of the studios.

LUCAS: The film is owned by the studio, and in the United States if you own something you can do anything you want with it.

EBERT: So the creator, i.e., the director, under American law has no power to prevent them from cutting it up in any way they want, colorizing it, shortening it, cropping it.

LUCAS: The thing that happened is a perversion of copyright idea. Copyright was originally developed by writers to protect their work from other people coming in and re-editing and changing it and rewriting it. So that if James Joyce decided to write whatever he wrote, and he wrote it, and that's what it was, you couldn't come along later and change it and then say, "Because it's too hard to understand, we'll change it and it will still be James Joyce's *Portrait of an Artist.*" It doesn't work that way. In publishing in most cases the artist actually owns the copyright. But in film it doesn't work that way. And what's happening in most of the countries around the world is that people have accepted the fact that the writer/director is basically the creative artist involved and have allowed him to continue to have those rights, which is called the "moral rights of artists," so that if their name is on something it should be their work and not somebody else's work. In the United States they don't believe that, because of the fact that basically if you buy something you can change it.

EBERT: Which is what the studios are doing.

LUCAS: That's what the studios are doing, and then they say, "This is *that* movie!" And it doesn't say anything about the fact that it's been altered or changed.

EBERT: Part of this is a process of education. For example, the process of telling people or hoping to convince people that they should want to see a black and white movie in black and white, which most people don't. Most people apparently feel they'd just as soon see it colorized.

LUCAS: Well, imagine the same thing with *Ulysses*. If you could bring out an easier-to-read version of *Ulysses* and most of the people in this society were literate—which is not really possible right now!—they would probably say, "Gee, I like this version better. It's much easier to read." And you'd have a hard time selling the original version. But the whole point would probably be lost and it'd be watered down and it wouldn't be anything like the experience that James Joyce originally intended it to be. And his reputation and the art and the contribution to the civilization would have been lost.

EBERT: When the Directors Guild was testifying before Congress and so forth, one of the arguments that was brought up that I thought had some validity to it was, "Why are the directors so concerned about their movies being shortened in length, when they're almost always shortened in width by being shown on television? Why is it more important that we not lose ten minutes of your film than that we not lose 40 percent of it because it isn't letterboxed?"

LUCAS: Yeah, but the directors are also saying that they want it let-

terboxed and they don't want commercials and they don't want
it shortened and they don't want it colorized. They want it to
be shown the way it was originally projected in the theater.
Obviously that, in the real world, is not possible. It will be
eventually, but what they're saying basically is that there should
be a law that says if they're going to make changes they go to
the director and writer and say, "Is it all right if we do this? Is it
all right if we cut off the sides? Is it all right if we shorten it? Is
it all right if we colorize it? Is it all right . . ." And to have that
person make the decision and say, "I realize this. I want to make
the money. Okay, go ahead and do it." Or, "No way! I don't want
my film seen that way and I want it to stay just the way it is and I
don't want to see it on television."

EBERT: When I was in Steven Spielberg's office last September
I visited him on a day when he was looking at the cropped
versus the letterboxed versions of *Last Crusade,* and he finally
slammed his fist down on the table and he said, "Tell them I'm
going to release it letterboxed in all versions. Just do it, and that's
it." But it didn't happen that way. It's available letterboxed in all
versions and indeed in disc the letterboxed version is outselling
the other four to one. But nevertheless it was released cropped,
also. Do the studios feel that strongly that they must do this?

LUCAS: There's a large argument that says that it has to be that way
at this point, and Steve acquiesced. It wasn't that we did it over
Steve's objection, but Steve is a reasonable person and he realized
that if you cut two-thirds of your cassette markets out you're
losing vast sums of money. And then you begin to say, "Well, as
long as I can have it in letterbox in all forms and the other thing, it
will be okay, because then the people can choose." And we de-
manded that they promote the letterbox and do a big deal on it.
Ultimately people are reasonable when it gets down to it. But you
have to sort of push to even get it released in letterbox at all.

EBERT: And then the sales figures for laser disc were, I think, enlight-
ening to Paramount.

LUCAS: Yeah.

EBERT: They didn't expect it to go that way.

LUCAS: Yeah. No, and I think that every time you do it they get a little bit more knowledge and it pushes that idea a little bit further. All the studios, everybody is terrified of artists' rights. And the truth of it is, most artists are very reasonable people and it wouldn't change anything. All it would do is, it would protect some of our heritage from somebody coming in—and it could be anyone—and completely destroying four or five thousand movies and just completely changing them to anything they wanted to do. They have the power to do that, and it's legal. All we're saying is, that shouldn't be legal. The artist who created it should have some say in it since his name's on it. And then there's this other, more extreme problem, which is the films should be preserved in their original condition. We shouldn't lose them. Because what they're doing is they're losing them to indifference and then they're being altered for momentary financial concerns without any regard to whether the emotional experience remains intact. That's the other issue: A movie is not as good on television as it is in a movie theater because a movie's a continuous experience. It's designed to be that way. It's designed for you to sit down and watch it for two hours and then get up and . . .

EBERT: . . . and walk away.

LUCAS: All this stuff accumulates and builds. It's a dramatic structure. Sometimes you can write an intermission in, but you just can't get up every ten minutes and wander around and come back and sit down and have the same experience as it was originally intended.

EBERT: And read the paper at the same time and talk to your family.

LUCAS: Yeah. I mean that's the audience's prerogative to do those sorts of things, but they shouldn't be forced to sit and look at something that's been chopped up and squeezed.

EBERT: I had a conversation with Milos Forman a couple of months ago that amazed me, because he confessed—and he said he knew he shouldn't say this—that he doesn't like letterboxing. He says, "Those black bands at the top and bottom of the screen simply distract me."

LUCAS: Right.

EBERT: Most people would agree with him, or a lot of people.

LUCAS: All artists' rights are saying is that it's the filmmaker's decision. Milos's films wouldn't be done that way. He'd say, "I'd rather have it be moved back and forth."

EBERT: So that's *his* choice.

LUCAS: Ideally what you want to do, which is what HDTV is getting toward, is wide-screen television.

EBERT: And then will they chop off the tops and bottoms of pre-1953 movies?

LUCAS: I don't know. They'll probably have blank things on the side.

EBERT: Somehow those things on the side won't bother people as much.

LUCAS: They don't bother you as much as this way.

EBERT: Because what's left is what you're used to looking at.

LUCAS: Right. It's like speakers on the side or something. Yeah. And I know the high definition television now is pretty close to 1.85.

EBERT: So even a 2.35:1 picture could be letterboxed in a reasonable way.

LUCAS: Yeah, the bands would be much, much less. And I think eventually they'll bring it all the way out. Because you go this way it's much easier. And once the whole idea of large screen television, high definition, and quality comes into it, somebody will offer it. And if that sells then it will become "the thing" and then there's the marketplace to consider. But I think people would like to see nice, large screens in their homes and see films the way they were intended.

March 30, 1990

AFTERWORD
BY GENE SISKEL

I have a couple of reactions to rereading these interviews. First, I owe thanks to Martin Scorsese for introducing me to the concept of "the master image," the one image that sums up a film or, as I would like to extrapolate here, a career.

That question provided the best answers in these sessions: Scorsese's "boxing ring of life," Spielberg's "door of light," and Lucas's rocket-rapid pacing.

Were you let down by Lucas's answer? Don't be. I think it's just as revealing as the other two. As a youth, Lucas was a car freak and drag racer. Indeed, his life was akin to Paul LeMat's dragster character in *American Graffiti*. And that thrill of the chase, the pursuit of the speed-freak's high, is communicated best in the outer-space drag race that concludes the first *Star Wars*.

One revision. I ran into Scorsese in May 1990 at the Cannes Film Festival. It was one in the morning in the lobby bar at the Hotel du Cap. The first thing out of his excitable mouth: "I thought of a better answer to that question about who was the happiest character in one of my films." (His original answer: Rupert Pupkin in *The King of Comedy*.)

"It's so obvious," Scorsese said. "It's Jesus (in *The Last Temptation of Christ*)."

At press time, February 1991, each of these directors is at work on a new film—Scorsese on a remake of *Cape Fear*; Spielberg, that remake of *Peter Pan* he talked so much about during the interview; and Lucas is producing a drama about World War II black airmen as well as a "young Indiana Jones" TV show.

Okay, so originality is not one of the long suits of the American movie industry as the first century of film concludes.

What will take us out of this tailspin in which movies seem to be shrinking in size and spirit to become little more than oversized television?

In a fine 1979 book called *The Movie Brats,* Michael Pye and Lynda Myles profiled six filmmakers who were among the first wave of film school graduates and who had come to prominence in the 1970s. Scorsese, Lucas, and Spielberg were in the group along with Francis Coppola, Brian De Palma, and John Milius.

The authors argued that the film revolution these directors participated in grew out of social changes in the culture itself. That makes sense.

And so, believing that the past is prelude, if you want my prediction about the future of the movies, I believe things will not get better or more exciting until we have some good old-fashioned upheaval in this country and the world beyond.

Somewhere, right now, perhaps reading this book, there is a young film student who views the later work of our three directors as tired, as complacent, as the work of the establishment.

That person is the future of the movies.